I0804945

# A WOMAN'S *faith*

*from the Marta Maria Podcast*

Leticia Mottola Araujo
Ana Carolina de Castro
Laís Carvalho Gonçalves
Caroline Melazzo

# A WOMAN'S *faith*

CFI
An imprint of Cedar Fort, Inc.
Springville, Utah

Paperback ISBN 13: 978-1-4621-4979-7
eBook ISBN 13: 978-1-4621-4980-3

Published by CFI, an imprint of Cedar Fort, Inc.
2373 W. 700 S., Suite 100, Springville, UT 84663
Distributed by Cedar Fort, Inc., www.cedarfort.com

Library of Congress Cataloging Number: 2025944321

Cover design by Shawnda Craig
Cover design © 2025 Cedar Fort, Inc.
Edited by Kyle Lund
Typeset by Liz Kazandzhy

Printed in the United States of America

10 9 8 7 6 5 4 3 2 1

Printed on acid-free paper

To my forever babies: Julian and Zoë Caroline.
Your mother knew.
*Ana Caroline de Castro*

To my beloved husband, sons, parents (in loving memory), and siblings—thank you for being my family and for walking with me in Christ's light and truth. With all my love.
*Caroline Melazzo*

To my husband and children, who teach me daily what love and faith look like.
And to every reader seeking hope, may you feel the Savior walking with you.
*Laís Carvalho Gonçalves*

To my children—may you always know how deeply you are loved by your Heavenly Father.
And to my amazing husband—your unwavering support has carried me more times than I can count.
*Leticia Mottola Araujo*

# Contents

# Introduction

Do you find yourself connecting everyday moments to scripture? Maybe a movie reminds you of a Bible story, or a song stirs a memory of a powerful verse. Perhaps, in a moment of doubt or decision, you instinctively turn to the scriptures for guidance, searching for reassurance and wisdom. If any of this sounds familiar, you're already living the scriptures—maybe without even realizing it!

Living the scriptures isn't about memorizing every verse or decoding ancient languages. It's about seeing God's word alive in your daily life. It's about recognizing the same God who parted the Red Sea, fed the five thousand, and comforted the Nephites is speaking to *you*, right here, right now.

We—Ana, Carol, Letícia, and Laís—have spent years trying to balance faith with everyday life. That's exactly why we created the *Marta Maria Podcast*. Marta and Maria are the Portuguese names for Martha and Mary in the New Testament. We all remember Mary—praised by Jesus for choosing "the good part," sitting at His feet and learning. But what about Martha? The one busy with the daily, never-ending tasks of life? Kids to care for, laundry to wash (and fold—ugh, the worst!), meals to cook, and then cleaning, cleaning, and more cleaning. *It never ends.*

That's what the *Marta Maria Podcast* is all about: bridging the gap between the spiritual and the practical. Faith isn't just found in deep study or quiet prayer. It's woven into the *messy, everyday reality* of our lives. We created this podcast after noticing a lack of gospel-centered content in our native language, Portuguese. We wanted a space where women could come together, share real-life struggles, and connect with scripture in meaningful ways.

Nothing makes us happier than when one of our listeners comments on a video, saying they listened to an episode while doing the dishes. Way to live the good part *and* the boring part at the same time! That's the kind of God we have—one who loves us, sees us, and meets us right where we are.

He comes to us in the most mundane moments if we're aligned to Him. Think about it; how many times have you been driving, and a hymn or a scripture came to mind? or folding laundry when you suddenly felt prompted to reach out to someone? That's Him. That's God, speaking to you.

And that's why we do what we do, to help us focus on those moments, learning to recognize when God is speaking to us individually. Each week on the *Marta Maria Podcast*, we dive into gospel discussions that add to our personal scripture study, helping us all connect the word of God to our real, everyday lives. Our episodes follow the *Come, Follow Me* curriculum, providing insights and conversations to strengthen faith. But make no mistake—nothing can replace the power of going directly to the source: the scriptures.

This book is an extension of those conversations—full of personal stories, real struggles, and scriptural insights. Each chapter includes experiences that have shaped our faith, practical ways to apply gospel principles, and thoughtful questions to help you reflect on your own journey.

# Part I

# Foundations of Practical Faith

# 1
# Living Scripture Daily

THE SUMMER OF 1999 WAS UNFORGETTABLE FOR MY FAMILY. WITH its pristine beaches and impressive sand dunes, Fortaleza, Brazil, was everything we had dreamed of for our long-anticipated vacation. My siblings, Henry and Jacqueline, and I, full of teenage energy, eagerly embraced every adventure the trip offered. One day, we boarded a dune buggy for a famous ride through the breathtaking dunes.

With a grin, the guide asked us, "With or without emotion?" Naturally, we chose *emotion*. The buggy roared to life, soaring over the dunes, twisting and dropping with exhilarating speed. The wind rushed past us, the sun warmed our faces, and the sand shimmered like gold. Each turn felt like a moment suspended in time, full of joy and anticipation. The ride culminated at the "butt slide," a massive dune where visitors could slide down its sandy slope on their backsides.

Henry, Jacqueline, and I raced each other down, laughing freely and wholeheartedly. Each trip was faster and more thrilling than the last. But suddenly, on one of my runs, everything went dark. I passed out, slipping into a stillness that felt like eternity, as though time itself had stopped. It felt like I was dreaming. Time, space, and awareness all blurred together into a strange sensation.

Suddenly, I awoke and found myself lying on the warm sand. My father knelt beside me, his hands gently on my head as he concluded a priesthood blessing: "In the name of Jesus Christ, Amen." I realized I was lying in the shade of a large *tenda de sapê*—a simple lounge area nestled within the dunes, covered with woven palm leaves to provide relief from the sun. This spot, a resting place for adventurers like us, held a few bottles of water and other small comforts for the journey. My family was gathered around me, their expressions a mix of relief and worry, while a couple of locals nearby looked on, their faces kind and reassuring.

Someone placed a freshly opened coconut in my hands. The cold, sweet water inside contrasted with the dry heat of the dunes, its taste, soothing and refreshing, spread through my body. I sipped slowly, the cool liquid reviving me further, as I sat propped up on the warm sand in the shaded shelter.

It wasn't just the coconut water that brought comfort; it was everything around me: my family, the concerned onlookers, and their willingness to help us in this moment of despair. While I was recovering and drinking the coconut water, my mother pulled me into a tight embrace, her voice trembling as she said, "You passed out. We were so scared."

At that moment, I felt something profound: God's unmistakable presence. Doctrine and Covenants 84:88 came to mind: "And whoso receiveth you, there I will be also, for I will go before your face. I will be on your right hand and on your left, and my Spirit shall be in your hearts, and mine angels round about you, to bear you up." That scripture captured exactly what I felt at that moment, a sense of being lifted, protected, and surrounded by divine love.

This realization became even more meaningful when I considered where we were—miles from the city, surrounded by towering dunes in what felt like the middle of nowhere. There was no immediate help available, no nearby hospitals or emergency responders. What my parents relied on at that moment was not the resources of the earth but the power of heaven. My father's priesthood blessing, uttered with faith and authority, bridged our need on earth with the divine help of heaven.

This connection between earth and heaven is a central truth of the gospel. God has provided us with tools and channels enabling us to access His power: prayer, scripture, faith, and ordinances through the priesthood. These are not abstract ideas; they are real, tangible, and designed to help us navigate the challenges of mortality. When we make the effort to engage in these channels, the veil between heaven and earth becomes thinner, and miracles happen. It's not that heaven suddenly intervenes, rather we align ourselves with heaven, inviting divine power into our lives.

One of the most powerful tools we have is the word of God. The scriptures are far more than an ancient record; they are alive, relevant, and offer guidance and strength for every moment of our lives. My mother was a living testament to this truth. Growing up, she taught us to see the scriptures as a personal letter from God to His children. She reminded us that every story, every teaching, and every promise in the scriptures has relevance to our lives today. Through her example, I learned that the scriptures can be both a source of power and a shield, fortifying us against life's challenges.

That day on the dunes, the scripture from Doctrine and Covenants 84:88 wasn't just a verse I had memorized. It was a truth I had internalized. My parents had taught me to see scripture as more than words on a page. They encouraged me to live scripture daily, to let them shape my thoughts and guide my actions. It wasn't a passive exercise, but an active process of applying the lessons and promises of God's word to my everyday life. "Seek ye first the kingdom of God, and his righteousness; and all these things shall be added unto you"[1] became our family motto, guiding countless decisions big and small. I remember as a young girl being invited to an exciting event on a Sunday, but I had already made the decision to honor the Sabbath. Though it was difficult to say no, I remembered that promise. Later, even better opportunities followed—ones that didn't conflict with my values. It was a small but powerful reminder that when we put God

1. Matthew 6:33.

first, He truly provides all that we need—just as He promised to add "all these things" unto us.

My father's priesthood blessing over me that day was simple yet powerful. It wasn't his words that made the difference—it was the faith behind them. Through prayer, my father called upon the power of heaven to intervene on earth, and I felt the reality of that power in the peace and strength that followed. But the foundation for that moment had been laid long before, through years of living scripture as a family.

Living scripture daily means seeing it as a living, breathing guide for the challenges we face. It means building a relationship with Christ so that, like my mother taught us, we can draw on its power when we need it most. For example, years later, when both of my parents became ill at the same time—each with different and serious diseases—it was one of the hardest seasons our family had ever faced. But because we had spent years rooted in the scriptures, they became our source of strength. Hope, comfort, and love weren't distant ideals; they were tangible realities we felt in the middle of our trials. We prayed together constantly. We leaned on God's promises as we took turns accompanying them to appointments, coordinating hospital visits, and managing treatments. The Word gave us direction, and more than that, it gave us peace. We didn't just read the scriptures—we lived them. And in return, they carried us. God's promises are real, and His words have the power to shape our hearts and actions.

The dunes that day symbolized life: its peaks of joy and sudden drops into darkness. Like the moment I passed out, challenges often come without warning. But because my parents had taught me to rely on scripture, prayer, and faith, I was prepared. Years later, when other trials came into my life—disappointments, heartbreak, or loss—I leaned on those same promises. Doctrine and Covenants 84:88 came back to me again and again, as if God were whispering directly to my heart: "I am here. I will bear you up." Living scripture daily doesn't mean life will be free of challenges, but it means we are never alone when we face them.

To live scripture daily, we must go beyond reading—we must ponder and apply it. Let the words become part of who you are, influencing your choices, strengthening your faith, and giving you courage in trials. My mother often asked us after family scripture study, "What does this mean for you today?" Her question taught me that scripture is a conversation between us and God, and that its lessons are meant to be lived, not just understood.

President Marion G. Romney once said: "I feel certain that if, in our homes, parents will read from the Book of Mormon prayerfully and regularly, both by themselves and with their children, the spirit of that great book will come to permeate our homes and all who dwell therein. The spirit of reverence will increase; mutual respect and consideration for each other will grow. The spirit of contention will depart. Parents will counsel their children in greater love and wisdom. Children will be more responsive and submissive to the counsel of their parents. Righteousness will increase. Faith, hope, and charity—the pure love of Christ—will abound in our homes and lives, bringing in their wake peace, joy, and happiness."[2] This powerful truth reminds us that studying the scriptures daily brings divine guidance into every facet of our lives, helping us navigate life's unexpected dunes with faith and confidence.

Prayer and scripture work hand in hand. Prayer allows us to speak to God, while scripture gives Him a way to speak back to us. When we combine these practices, we open ourselves to His direction and power in a way that transforms our hearts and strengthens our resolve.

When we use the tools God has given us—scriptures, prayer, faith, ordinances—we invite His presence into our lives. We align earth with heaven, opening the way for miracles, peace, and strength.

*Caroline Melazzo*

## Questions to Ponder

I encourage you to reflect on your own life:

- How has God gone before you?
- When have His angels borne you up?

This week, study Doctrine and Covenants 84:88 and consider writing down one scripture each morning that resonates with you.

---

2. Marion G. Romney, "The Book of Mormon," *Ensign*, May 1980, 67.

Think about how you can apply it to your day. Pair your scripture study with a prayer for understanding, and watch as God's words shape your actions and bring clarity to your challenges.

Living scripture daily means believing that God's words are for *you*. They are alive and real. They have the power to comfort, guide, and transform you. That summer in Fortaleza taught me this truth in a profound way: God's promises are real, and He is always near. His angels bore me up that day—through my father's blessing, my mother's embrace, and the truths they instilled in me.

When we choose to live scripture daily, we invite the power of God's word to shape our lives, fill our hearts with peace, and carry us through even the most unexpected moments.

# 2

# The Role of Faith and Action

## Balancing Belief and Practice in the Application of Scripture

I WAS STANDING AT A CROSSROADS. IN JANUARY 2010, I HAD JUST graduated from high school and found myself with a blank slate and no clear direction. My older siblings had taken a clear path before me: They both went to BYU in the United States for their undergraduate studies. Naturally, I planned to follow in their footsteps. Yet, when the time came for me to begin the application process, doubt crept in. Was I prepared? Was this even the right path for me?

The application forms for BYU were in my hands. I'd started filling them out and was ready to complete them, but something was holding me back. I felt a strange lack of peace, which was unusual for me. I had always been so sure of what I wanted, but this time, I hesitated. "Why don't I feel good about this?" I asked myself.

Simultaneously, I couldn't ignore the doubts I had about staying in Brazil. I hadn't prepared for the *vestibular*—a challenging series of entrance exams required by Brazilian universities. While all my classmates had spent years preparing for these exams, I had focused solely on applying to BYU, confident that my future was abroad. Now, that confidence wavered.

During this time of confusion, my aunt reached out with an unexpected invitation. She lived in Goiânia, a city far from where I was raised. She suggested I come live with her for a few months. "Come figure things out," she said. "There are some good courses you can study nearby before college starts. Come explore your options!"

I wasn't entirely sure how living with my aunt would help me, but something in her offer felt right. I packed my bags and moved in with her and her family, ready to see where this new chapter would lead.

Shortly after arriving in Goiânia, I stumbled upon a graphic design course. It was practical, hands-on, and completely unlike anything I had considered before. On impulse, I signed up. The course sparked something in me—a sense of excitement and creativity I hadn't felt in years.

For the first time, I began to consider the possibility of staying in Brazil to pursue higher education. One night, after weeks of reading the scriptures daily, wondering and praying about what to do, a verse from the Book of Mormon stood out to me: "Counsel with the Lord in all thy doings, and he will direct thee for good" (Alma 37:37).

I knelt down to pray. "Heavenly Father," I said, "I don't know what to do. Should I stay in Brazil? Should I pursue graphic design here? Please help me know what you want for me."

Almost immediately, I felt a prompting: "Go to the computer and search for graphic design schools in Brazil." It was late at night, and I hesitated. The thought seemed so simple, almost trivial. But the impression came again, stronger this time: "Get up. Go to the computer."

I obeyed.

That small act of faith—getting up and searching for schools—led to one of the most significant revelations of my life. Within minutes, I found several universities offering graphic design programs, and one school in particular stood out immediately: ESPM—it was the very first option I saw. As I explored their website, excitement bubbled up inside me. *This is it!* I thought. *This is the right path!*

At the time, I thought the decision to stay in Brazil was simply about my education and future career. But now I see that the Lord's guidance was about so much more. By remaining in Brazil, I was able to spend my mother's last years by her side as she battled cancer. I was there to hold her hand during treatments, to laugh with her on the good days, and to cherish every moment we had together.

Miraculously, the Lord also led both my brother and sister back to Brazil during this same time. My brother returned in June 2013, and my sister in September 2011. As a family, we were all together during her final year, unified and at peace as she passed into the next life. It's impossible for me to separate these blessings from the Lord's hand. While I didn't fully understand the reasons behind His prompting me to stay in Brazil back in 2010, looking back, it's clear. He had a greater plan—a plan to strengthen and unify our family during one of the most sacred and challenging times of our lives.

That small act of faith—searching for schools and eventually choosing to stay in Brazil, trusting the Lord's prompting—was about much more than my education. Through this experience, I learned that God's answers to our prayers often hold layers of meaning we can only understand with time.

What seemed like a decision about my education turned out to be part of a much larger blessing—bringing my family together in a way only He could orchestrate. My choice to stay in Brazil allowed me to be present with my mother in her final years, a gift I will always treasure.

I also learned that when we follow promptings, even without knowing the full picture, the Lord's plan will always work for our good. God rarely hands us the full blueprint of His plan all at once. Instead, He gives us small, actionable steps, trusting that we'll have the faith to follow His promptings.

Faith and action go hand in hand. Believing in God's plan is vital, but belief must be accompanied by effort. The scriptures repeatedly teach this principle:

- "Faith, if it hath not works, is dead" (James 2:17).
- "Seek, and ye shall find; knock, and it shall be opened unto you" (Matthew 7:7).

When we face uncertainty or major decisions, it's easy to feel overwhelmed. We might wonder, "What if I make the wrong choice? What if I don't hear the answer?" But the truth is, God often speaks to us through small promptings, like the one I received to search for schools late at night. Acting on those promptings, even when they seem insignificant, demonstrates our trust in Him.

Here are three practical takeaways from my experience:

1. **Pray with the intention to act.** When you ask God for guidance, be ready to take the next step—even if you don't have all the answers yet.
2. **Start small.** Often, the first step toward clarity is simple: make a phone call, research online, or talk to someone you trust.
3. **Trust the process.** Revelation doesn't always come immediately, but as you move forward in faith, the path will unfold in ways you didn't expect.

Think about a decision or challenge you're currently facing. Maybe it's choosing a career, starting a family, or navigating a difficult relationship. Whatever it is, I invite you to take these steps:

1. **Counsel with the Lord.** Spend time in prayer and scripture study, asking for His guidance.
2. **Take one actionable step.** Write down a small, specific action you can take today to move forward.
3. **Trust the outcome to God.** Remember that you don't need to have everything figured out. As long as you're moving forward with faith and effort, the Lord will guide you.

Looking back, I see how God's hand was in every detail of my decision to stay in Brazil and study graphic design. That experience set the stage for countless blessings in my life, from my educational growth to the sacred opportunity of being with my family during my mother's final years.

*Letícia Araujo*

# 3

# Scripture as a Guidebook for Modern Life

## Adapting Ancient Wisdom to Contemporary Challenges

I WAS AT THE END OF MY MISSION WITH ONLY A COUPLE OF TRANSFERS left, which meant about three months until I would return home. Throughout my mission, I had always focused on the work—being present in the moment and doing what needed to be done. I often spoke with other sisters who would share stories about their boyfriends or the guys they were exchanging letters with. I was genuinely happy for them, but I didn't feel the same need to think about my future in that way.

I wasn't worried about when I would get married or if it would happen at all. I had a deep confidence that marriage would come when it was meant to. I wasn't impatient, nor did I feel like I needed clarity about my future. I knew things like returning to school, buying a car, and eventually starting a family would happen in due time. My mission was my focus, and I trusted in God's timing for everything else.

But in His infinite wisdom, God works in ways we don't expect. Even though I wasn't asking or searching for direction about my future, He gave me a glimpse of something that I didn't realize I needed. It was an ordinary evening at the end of December—hot and humid, as summers in Cuiabá, Brazil, always were. The days between Christmas and New Year's had been especially rewarding. People seemed more open to hearing about Christ, and I felt a special spirit in the air as we taught and shared His message.

After a long day of work, my companion and I returned home. I followed my usual routine—showering, eating, planning for the next day, and then heading to bed. But that night, something unusual happened. I woke up in the middle of the night, wide awake, and unable to go back to sleep. Normally, I was so exhausted that once my head hit the pillow, I was out until the alarm rang. But this night was different.

As I lay in my bed, I saw myself standing in front of the São Paulo Temple. I was dressed in white, and as I looked around, I saw two very dear friends who had become an eternal couple, along with a childhood friend who was also a member of the Church. We were all filled with joy, smiling and laughing together. The scene felt peaceful, warm, and sacred. My heart overflowed with love, peace, and joy—a deep, overwhelming sense that I was exactly where I was meant to be.

The experience was vivid in every way. It felt so real. I could feel the warmth of the weather on my skin, the gentle breeze that carried the scent of flowers from the vibrant flower beds surrounding the temple. The beautiful palm trees swayed nearby, framing the temple in such a majestic way. I could hear the soothing sound of water cascading from the temple's fountain, adding to the tranquility of the moment. It was as if every detail was designed to assure me of the love and perfection of God's plans.

When the vision ended, I felt an undeniable urge to write down everything I had felt and seen. I grabbed my journal and began pouring out my thoughts, doing my best to capture every detail and even my lingering questions. In that moment of inspiration, I wrote a letter to my future spouse. I didn't know who he would be, but I felt moved to express my love and to make personal commitments about how I wanted to treat him. As I wrote, the friend from my vision came to mind. For the first time, I began to wonder if there was something more to our friendship. I felt a deep love for him and recorded it, though I didn't yet understand whether that love could someday blossom into eternal love.

Just as I was finishing, completely unaware of the time, the alarm rang at 6:30 a.m. It was time to wake up. My companion stirred, prayed, and began to get ready for the day. I shared with her that I'd had a special and sacred experience that kept me awake through the night and asked if I could rest briefly before starting our busy day. It was Saturday, and we had to prepare those we were teaching to attend church the following day. I soon dove back into the work, but the vision remained with me, lingering in my mind and heart.

As the day went on, I couldn't help but question the meaning of the experience. Was this a sign that I was supposed to marry my friend? or was it something else entirely? The words of President Henry B. Eyring from a talk I had heard earlier in my mission came to my mind: "Plead that the Spirit will show you what the Lord wants you to do. Plan to do it. Promise Him to obey. Act with determination until you have done what He asked. And then pray to give thanks for the opportunity to serve and to know what you might do next."[3] At the time, I had understood this counsel in the context of missionary work—finding people to teach and following spiritual promptings. But now, those words felt deeply personal, as if God Himself were gently speaking to me.

I wasn't consumed by figuring everything out immediately. I just wanted to know if the experience was truly from God. If it was, I knew I could trust that He had a purpose in revealing it to me. I turned to the scriptures for guidance, seeking confirmation and clarity. That day, I came across Galatians 5:22: "But the fruit of the Spirit is love, joy, peace, longsuffering, gentleness, goodness, faith."

This verse spoke directly to my heart. It confirmed that the feelings I had experienced during the vision—and as the day unfolded—were indeed fruits of the Spirit. Peace, love, and joy surrounded me in a way that could only come from God. It was His way of assuring

3. Henry B. Eyring, *Act in All Diligence*, General Conference (Salt Lake City; The Church of Jesus Christ of Latter-day Saints), April 2010, Gospel Library App.

me that the experience was not random or imagined; it was inspired. With that knowledge, I felt deeply reassured and resolved to trust Him with whatever lay ahead.

The realization brought me profound peace. I didn't have to worry about what the future held. I didn't need to know all the answers right then. The Lord had given me enough light to take the next step. He had shown me the potential for something beautiful, and now it was up to me to trust Him and move forward in faith.

As it often happens with God's gentle workings, something remarkable unfolded just after that sacred experience. On Monday morning, the first email I saw in my inbox was from the friend I saw standing next to me in my vision. It had been a long time since we last spoke, and seeing his name surprised me. I remember looking up at the sky and thinking, *I just spoke with Thee about waiting a little longer.* It was as if God was saying, "Here's the next step."

When I returned home from my mission, our paths crossed again. Though he was living abroad at the time, he came to visit his family, and we reconnected. We began spending time together, going on a few dates, and I started to see him with fresh eyes. I didn't feel the Lord was telling me to "Marry him," rather, "Take the time to get to know him better and see the possibilities." The Spirit showed me that there was a beautiful potential for happiness if I chose to explore this path, but the decision would always be mine.

The Lord loves us enough to guide us gently, presenting us with possibilities while trusting us to make our own choices. For that, I am deeply grateful.

Over time, I got to know him in a new and deeper way. I began to notice qualities I hadn't fully appreciated before—his kindness, his faith, and a quiet strength that I admired deeply. Six months later, we were married and sealed in the temple. Now, ten years later, I look back with gratitude for how the Lord gently led me, never forcing a decision but showing me beautiful possibilities. He knew what I needed, even when I wasn't asking for it, and for that, I am forever thankful.

This experience taught me that God truly knows us individually. Even when we're not asking, even when we think we don't need anything, He is aware of us. He knows what we need, when we need it, and how to reveal it in a way that helps us grow. The scriptures became my greatest guide during this process, helping me recognize the fruits of the Spirit as confirmation of divine guidance. They reassured me that God's promises are true—that as we seek first His kingdom, He will show us the way forward and provide for everything else along the way.

*Laís Gonçalves*

## Questions to Ponder

- Think about a time when the Lord gently guided you toward a decision or a new path. How did His guidance help you see possibilities you hadn't considered before?
- How can you use the scriptures as a guide in your life to recognize the Lord's hand and find peace in times of uncertainty?
- What experiences have taught you to trust God's timing and the gentle ways He works in your life? How can you strengthen that trust moving forward?

# 4

# Hearing God's Voice Through Scripture

RIGHT NOW, AS I WRITE THIS, I'M IN THE MIDDLE OF THE HARDEST experience of my life: a divorce.

If you had told me years ago that I'd be here, I wouldn't have believed you. I've always been the girl who *dreamed* of marriage—being a wife, a mom, and living that classic white-picket-fence life. And for a while, I had it. Two years after my mission, I got married, had kids, and from the outside, everything looked perfect. But behind closed doors? I was drowning.

For years, I tried to hold my marriage together through a season of deep struggle, I told myself that if I just prayed more, sacrificed more, loved harder, forgave deeper, and carried the weight for both of us, everything would eventually get better. But over time, I came to a painful realization: I couldn't change what was not mine to change. What I could change was my life—and reclaim my peace and happiness. And so, I faced the hardest decision of all: I had to let go. I had to start over.

I needed to choose my well-being. I needed to choose self-love. I needed to choose happiness. But more than anything, I needed to be a better and happier mom for my kids.

But *how*?

Divorce wasn't supposed to be part of my story. A family is what's best for kids, right? Divorce ruins kids, they say. You're sealed for eternity, they say. Marriage is hard, they say. You have to forgive, they say. This is what you signed up for, they say.

But what does *He* say?

For the last two years of my marriage, I pleaded with Heavenly Father for a clear answer. I begged Him to tell me what to do. But for the longest time, I felt like I got *nothing*.

Now, I'll be honest—I wasn't exactly making it easy to hear Him. I was so exhausted, so emotionally drained, that I stopped doing a lot of the things that usually kept me close to Him. I stopped going to the temple. I stopped reading my scriptures. I prayed, I cried, I begged—but I wasn't listening.

I grew up hearing, "If you want to talk to God, pray. If you want to hear God, read the scriptures."

I was only doing *half* of that equation.

Then one morning, I felt a strong desire to go to the temple. It was like something inside me *knew* I needed to be there. So, I called a friend, asked if she could watch my kids, and thankfully, she said yes.

Honestly? The whole drive there, I was tempted to just go do something easier. I thought about skipping the temple and going to the gym instead. Or wandering through a store alone. Or even just going home and taking a nap—because when you're depressed, a nap sounds like the best idea in the world.

But I pushed through and made it to the temple.

And let me tell you—*it was hard*.

I sat through the endowment session, listening to all the references to marriage, husbands, wives, and the law of chastity. Every mention of eternal families felt like a dagger to the heart. I felt like I *didn't belong* there anymore. I felt unworthy. I felt alone. I felt *angry*.

None of those feelings belong in the temple—but there I was, sitting with all of them.

As the session ended, and I made my way to the celestial room, I did what I have always done in the temple. I grabbed the scriptures. As I held the scriptures in my hand, I closed my eyes and said a heartfelt prayer. I asked God to remove these feelings from me. I asked for peace. I asked for reassurance. I asked for confirmation that I was making the right decision to get a divorce. I even told Him that I was willing to be unhappy for the rest of my life if it meant that my kids would be better off with their mom and dad married.

As soon as I said "Amen," it was like I was alone, and the celestial room went quiet. I know, I know, the celestial room is already quiet. But this was different. It felt like *everything* around me just *stilled.* I opened the scriptures in my hand, not seeking anything specific. The scriptures opened to Doctrine and Covenants 121, and the first thing I read was: "My son, peace be unto thy soul; thine adversity and thine afflictions shall be but a small moment; And then, if thou endure it well, God shall exalt thee on high; thou shalt triumph over all thy foes."[4]

As I read those words, they felt as though they were written directly to me. They weren't just words to Joseph Smith in Liberty Jail—they were for me.

Right there, in the middle of my storm, God was telling me: "I see you. I know how much you're hurting. And you don't have to suffer anymore."

I kept reading that section, and my absolute favorite verse stood out to me as well: "That the rights of the priesthood are inseparably connected with the powers of heaven, and that the powers of heaven cannot be controlled nor handled only upon the principles of righteousness."[5]

In that moment, it felt like God was crystal clear with me.

Though the priesthood was present in our home, our marriage wasn't aligned with the powers of heaven. Not because marriage—or the priesthood—isn't sacred, but because the foundation wasn't rooted in spiritual unity or on principles of righteousness. I was doing my best to honor my covenants, but over time, repeated disappointments left me at a crossroads. It didn't feel like a matter of free will anymore. It felt like a call to choose peace. I had to make a decision.

4. Doctrine and Covenants 121:7–8.

5. Doctrine and Covenants 121:36.

And for the first time, I felt *peace.*

God wasn't asking me to endure more. He wasn't asking me to keep suffering. He was giving me permission to *walk away*—and reassuring me that I would be okay.

Divorce would be hard, yes, but if I endured it well, I would triumph with the help of my personal Savior, Jesus Christ.

The story doesn't end there. I left the temple feeling such a sense of relief, determination, and even hope. But of course, Satan wasn't about to let me feel that peace for long. When I got into the car and started driving, doubts started to flood my mind.

*Maybe I read the scripture wrong.*

*Maybe 'endure it well' means I need to stay and keep suffering.*

*Maybe I misunderstood what God was trying to tell me.*

As soon as I turned right, just off the temple grounds, I saw a street sign.

The name of the street was "Y Worry Lane."

No joke.

Just like in the celestial room, it felt like I was alone on the road and the only thing I could see was that sign. God was again speaking directly to me. I had nothing to worry about as long as I followed the directions He had provided me and remained faithful to Him.

I will never forget this experience. I was in such a dark and hopeless place, but God shone His light on me again through the temple and, more specifically, through the scriptures. We often seek revelation in marvelous, dramatic ways, like seeing an angel or hearing an actual voice, but more often, it's about tuning our hearts and minds to recognize His presence in our lives through the scriptures. It's about making a sacrifice and showing God that we will put away all of our natural inclinations—not to pray, not to read, not to go to the temple—and many other impulses, just to commune with Him. Just to hear Him.

The scriptures became a lifeline for me during that time when I made the decision to leave my marriage, and they are still a lifeline right now as I'm going through the process. There have been numerous instances where God spoke directly to me about the struggles of divorcing through the scriptures. I learned that when we read the scriptures with an open heart and a prayerful spirit, God meets us in our specific needs and circumstances.

You may relate to my story about divorce, or maybe not. But I'm certain you've experienced—or will someday experience—moments of deep challenge. Life brings trials to all of us, each in different ways. Whatever your path looks like, the scriptures remain a source of comfort and guidance. They are not just ancient stories or verses to memorize; they are conversations to be had with your Heavenly Father—full of light, direction, and personal revelation.

Here are three takeaways from my experience:

1. **Open your scriptures.** Praying and pleading for help is not enough. We need to do all we can in order to connect with God. He hears us through prayers, and we hear Him through scriptures. If we don't seek His word, how can we expect to receive guidance? President Nelson said:

> The truths of the Book of Mormon have the *power* to heal, comfort, restore, succor, strengthen, console, and cheer our souls. My dear brothers and sisters, I promise that as you prayerfully study the Book of Mormon *every day*, you will make better decisions—*every day*. I promise that as you ponder what you study, the windows of heaven will open, and you will receive answers to your own questions and direction for your own life.[6]

2. **Listen to the promptings you receive.** When we feel promptings, like I did to go to the temple that day, we cannot ignore them. We need to push through whatever challenges we may have and follow through. If I had not gone to the temple, I wouldn't have opened the scriptures in the exact section, in the exact verse that I needed to read. The temple allowed the Spirit to be so strong in my heart and mind that I was able to receive revelation through the scriptures.
3. **Don't Doubt.** One of the biggest lessons I learned from The First Vision is that whenever something remarkable is about to happen, Satan will try to scare you into changing your mind. Just as I had left the temple, right after having received a per-

6. President Russell M. Nelson, *The Book of Mormon: What Would Your Life Be Like without It?*, General Conference (Salt Lake City: The Church of Jesus Christ of Latter-day Saints), October 2017, Gospel Library App.

> sonal revelation for my life, he tried to instill feelings of doubt and worry in me. Don't listen to him. Don't let doubt creep in. Your personal experiences with God, Jesus Christ and the Holy Ghost are real, and you know it.

As you face the storms in your life, remember that God's guidance is always available to you. President Nelson said, "In coming days, it will not be possible to survive spiritually without the guiding, directing, comforting, and constant influence of the Holy Ghost."[7] So open your heart, open your scriptures, and seek His word with faith and humility. Trust that He knows your struggles and will speak to you in ways that are deeply personal and uniquely meant for you. Through the scriptures, through prayer, and through the quiet promptings of the Spirit, you will find the strength, reassurance, and peace you need to move forward—one faithful step at a time.

*Ana de Castro*

## Questions to Ponder

- How have I experienced personal revelation in my own life, and what can I do to better recognize God's answers when they come?
- Are there any areas of my life where I might be hesitating to follow the promptings I've already received? What is holding me back?
- When have I doubted an answer I received from God, and how can I strengthen my faith to trust Him more fully?
- How have the scriptures provided me with comfort, clarity, or guidance in difficult times? How can I make them a more consistent source of revelation?
- What does it mean for me personally to "endure well" through challenges, and how can I rely on Christ to carry me through my trials?

---

7. President Russell M. Nelson, *Revelation for the Church, Revelation for Our Lives*, General Conference (Salt Lake City: The Church of Jesus Christ of Latter-day Saints), April 2018, Gospel Library App.

# Part II

# Scripture and Personal Growth

# 5

# Overcoming Fear, Anxiety, and Perfectionism

Let's just say it—I've always struggled with anxiety. Growing up, I felt like I had to be *everything*: the responsible one, the good one, the pretty one, the talented one. The one who had it all together. And honestly? That pressure only made my anxiety worse. I cared *way* too much about what people thought of me—and, if I'm being real, I still do.

Throw in religious expectations, and suddenly, it wasn't just about being a good person, it was about *being righteous enough*, *dressing modestly enough*, *saying the right things*, and *following every commandment with exactness.* And somewhere in all of that striving, I unknowingly slipped into the trap of perfectionism—the sneaky cousin of anxiety. Instead of finding peace in Christ, I became obsessed with checking all the right boxes and forgot *His grace* is what actually makes me whole.

Satan is an expert at twisting righteous desires into impossible burdens. He whispers that if we just work harder, sacrifice more, and discipline ourselves better, we can attain flawlessness. But this is a lie. The pursuit of perfectionism only leaves us exhausted, overwhelmed, and convinced that we are failing—because on our own, we always will.

The story of Jesus feeding the five thousand with just five loaves and two fish reminds me how the Savior operates.[8] The disciples looked at what they had and thought, *This is not enough. It's barely anything.* But Christ saw something different. He didn't ask them to perform a miracle; He simply asked them to bring what they had. He took their offering, blessed it, and multiplied it to be more than enough. Likewise, He asks us to come to Him with whatever we have, no matter how broken, weak, or inadequate it feels, and He will take over.

Contrast this with what Satan does. He tells us we must achieve perfection on our own. He insists that if we were more patient, more disciplined, more righteous, then we wouldn't struggle. He convinces us that if we fail to meet a certain standard, we are unworthy of peace, joy, or love. When we believe this lie, we chase impossible expectations—whether it's the perfect home, the perfect family, the perfect spiritual life, or the perfect body. And when we inevitably fall short, we feel like failures. This only adds to our stress and anxiety, causing us to try harder, and fall short again.

Can you see the cycle? It never ends. It just keeps us trapped in stress, guilt, and shame—right where Satan wants us.

I know this trap well. I lived in it for years. And honestly? I still fall into it from time to time. (Okay, *a lot of times.*) My anxiety has never been just about daily worries. It is tied to my sense of worth. I believed that if I wasn't constantly achieving, constantly performing, then I wasn't enough. But when my life crumbled in ways I never expected, I was forced to confront a hard truth: I could not carry this (or any) burden on my own. And the good news? I was never meant to.

In those dark moments, I turned to the scriptures. Honestly, at first it was just as a checklist item, because that's what I was taught to do. When life gets hard, we pray, and we read scriptures, right? But eventually, the scriptures became more to me. I craved them because

8. Matthew 14:13–21.

I needed real, living truth. I read about Christ's interactions with the broken, the weary, and the inadequate. In reading these accounts, I saw something I had never noticed before. His focus was never on how good they were. It was always on their willingness to come to Him. Time and again, He took what little they had and made it more.

Remember Peter walking on water?[9] He actually *did* it for a moment—until he got distracted by the storm. Then he started sinking, panic set in, and he cried, "Lord, save me!"

And what did Jesus do?

*Immediately*—not after a lecture, not after waiting for Peter to figure it out—*immediately*, He reached out and caught him.

He didn't say, "Wow, Peter, you really messed up there."

He just asked, "Why did you doubt?"

This story brings to mind two of my favorite paintings by Yongsung Kim. One, titled *The Hand of God*, captures this exact moment from Peter's perspective, emphasizing the Savior's unwavering reach. The other, *Rescue Me*, depicts Christ carrying someone from the depths of the sea, a powerful reminder that He does not just save us; He carries us when we cannot stand on our own.

That's the kind of Savior we have.

The One who tells us: "Come unto me, all ye that labour and are heavy laden, and I will give you rest."[10]

And if we come unto Him, we are given this powerful promise found in Moroni 10:32–33:

> Yea, come unto Christ, and be perfected in him, and deny yourselves of all ungodliness; and if ye shall deny yourselves of all ungodliness, and love God with all your might, mind and strength, then is his grace sufficient for you, that by his grace ye may be perfect in Christ; and if by the grace of God ye are perfect in Christ, ye can in nowise deny the power of God. And again, if ye by the grace of God are perfect in Christ, and deny not his power, then are ye sanctified in Christ by the grace of God, through the shedding of the blood of Christ, which is in the covenant of the Father unto the remission of your sins, that ye become holy, without spot.

---

9. Matthew 14:28–31.

10. Matthew 11:28.

Anxiety says we must work harder, do more, and be more to be at peace with ourselves and become perfect. Christ tells us to come to Him, let Him be our peace, and let Him make us perfect through His grace. The difference is profound.

For those of us who struggle with anxiety, depression, or any other mental health challenge, faith can feel like a double-edged sword. We may believe in Christ, yet we still feel afraid. We may know He is our Savior, yet we still feel broken. And then comes the guilt—*if I really trusted Christ, wouldn't I feel peace?* Elder Jeffrey R. Holland reminded us that struggling with mental health does not mean we lack faith:

> Though we may feel we are 'like a broken vessel,' as the Psalmist says, we must remember that vessel is in the hands of the divine potter. Broken minds can be healed just the way broken bones and broken hearts are healed. While God is at work making those repairs, the rest of us can help by being merciful, nonjudgmental, and kind.[11]

We *must* be kind to ourselves.

Christ never shamed those who struggled—He invited them in. And healing? Healing is a *process*. It doesn't mean we've failed.

Sometimes, the burden of not trusting Christ "enough" can add to our pain. If we struggle to believe, we may feel unworthy of His love. But faith isn't about achieving a perfect level of trust overnight. Faith grows as we keep coming to Christ, step by step. He asks us to take even the smallest steps toward Him, and He will meet us there.

Just as the Savior heals both body and soul, there are practical ways to calm our minds while we trust Him. Anxiety often grows from fear—fear of the unknown, fear of failure, or fear of rejection. Cognitive Behavioral Therapy (CBT) teaches that many anxious thoughts are distortions—beliefs that we are not enough, that we must control everything, or that disaster is certain. But just as Christ replaces Satan's lies with truth, we can replace these anxious distortions with the reality of His grace.

Some tools that can help include:

---

11. Jeffery R. Holland, *Like a Broken Vessel*, General Conference (Salt Lake City: The Church of Jesus Christ of Latter-day Saints), October 2013, Gospel Library App.

- **Mindfulness and Meditation**: Practicing mindfulness helps us stay present rather than getting lost in fears about the future. Meditation can also help quiet anxious thoughts and focus our minds on truth.
- **Breathing Techniques**: Simple deep breathing exercises can help calm the nervous system.
- **Journaling**: Writing down anxious thoughts and then challenging them with scripture and truth can be a powerful exercise.
- **Physical Activity**: Exercise has been shown to reduce symptoms of anxiety and depression. Even simple activities like walking can help.
- **Seeking Support**: Whether through professional counseling, support groups, or trusted friends and family, we are not meant to carry our burdens alone.

Spiritually, Christ is the ultimate antidote to our fears. He reminds us that we are enough because we are His. He reminds us that we are not alone. He will strengthen us, and His grace is sufficient.

So how do we overcome fear and anxiety? We replace the distorted belief with the truth.

Here are six examples of distorted beliefs and the truth to counter them through the scriptures:

"I have to be perfect to be worthy of God's love."

**Truth: God's love is unconditional. He loves us despite our imperfections.**

> For I am persuaded, that neither death, nor life, nor angels, nor principalities, nor powers, nor things present, nor things to come, Nor height, nor depth, nor any other creature, shall be able to separate us from the love of God, which is in Christ Jesus our Lord. (Romans 8:38–39).

"If I have enough faith, I won't struggle with trials, fear, or mental health challenges."

**Truth: Even the most faithful people in scripture faced hardships, doubt, and suffering. Faith does not remove struggles but helps us endure them.**

> And if men come unto me I will show unto them their weakness. I give unto men weakness that they may be humble; and my grace is sufficient for all men that humble themselves before me; for if they humble themselves before me, and have faith in me, then will I make weak things become strong unto them. (Ether 12:27).

"Repentance means I have to punish myself and feel guilty for a long time."

**Truth: Repentance is about change and healing, not self-condemnation.**

> Though your sins be as scarlet, they shall be as white as snow; though they be red like crimson, they shall be as wool. (Isaiah 1:18).

"God is disappointed in me because I struggle with doubt."

**Truth: Even prophets and apostles have experienced doubt[12]. God meets us where we are and helps us grow.**

> And straightway the father of the child cried out, and said with tears, Lord, I believe; help thou mine unbelief. (Mark 9:24).

"I have to earn grace."

**Truth: Grace is a gift, not something we earn. We show appreciation for it by striving to follow Christ.**

> For we labor diligently to write, to persuade our children, and also our brethren, to believe in Christ, and to be reconciled to God; for we know that it is by grace that we are saved, after all we can do. (2 Nephi 25:23).

"If I struggle with fear or anxiety, I must not be trusting God enough."

---

12. John 20:24–28.

**Truth: Trusting God does not mean never feeling fear. It means turning to Him *despite* our fears.**

> For God hath not given us the spirit of fear; but of power, and of love, and of a sound mind. (2 Timothy 1:7).

When we let go of the impossible expectation of perfection and instead turn to the Savior, we find true peace. Not the peace that comes from momentary success or external validation, but the peace that surpasses all understanding—the peace that only He can give.[13]

Elder Jeffrey R. Holland beautifully reassures us:

> Brothers and sisters, every one of us aspires to a more Christlike life than we often succeed in living. If we admit that honestly and are trying to improve, we are not hypocrites; we are human. May we refuse to let our own mortal follies, and the inevitable shortcomings of even the best men and women around us, make us cynical about the truths of the gospel, the truthfulness of the Church, our hope for our future, or the possibility of godliness. If we persevere, then somewhere in eternity our refinement will be finished and complete—which is the New Testament meaning of *perfection*.[14]

Anxiety remains a battle I face daily. I have sought professional help, and I continue to do so. Trust me, I see my therapist every week. I am not an expert on conquering anxiety and fear, but perhaps there is a reason I was meant to write this chapter—because I know what it feels like to be in the middle of the battle.

And maybe you needed to read this.

So let me tell you: You are enough, but not because you checked all the right boxes, because you never struggle, nor because you finally "fixed" yourself. You are enough because *you are His*.

If you find yourself in a similar struggle, please do not feel ashamed. Perhaps your battle looks different—whether it be depression, bipolar disorder, eating disorders, post-traumatic stress disorder, or something

---

13. Philippians 4:7.

14. Jeffrey R. Holland, *Be Ye Therefore Perfect—Eventually*, General Conference (Salt Lake City: The Church of Jesus Christ of Latter-day Saints), October 2017, Gospel Library App.

else entirely. Do not believe the cruel lie Satan whispers—that these struggles make you less than, or that they render you unworthy. The truth is we are more than our struggles, and through Christ, we can rise above them.

Perfection was never the goal—Christ is. The path to peace is not found in doing more, but in trusting more. When we stop chasing impossible expectations and start seeking the Savior, we realize something incredible: He has been running toward us all along.

*Ana de Castro*

## Questions to Ponder

- What areas of my life am I trying to control rather than trusting Christ?
- In what ways has Christ already carried me through difficult times?
- Are there any "distorted beliefs" in your life? List them and replace them with truths found in scriptures or in the words of our prophet and apostles.
- When have I felt the Savior reaching out to rescue me?
- What does it mean to me personally that His grace is sufficient?
- How can I apply mindfulness or other coping tools in moments of anxiety?
- How can I show myself the same compassion Christ offers me?

# 6

# Developing Discipline and Self-Control

## Practical Steps to Grow Spiritually and Personally

When I was six years old, I began gymnastics, and my world expanded to include early mornings, precise routines, and the thrill of progress. The alarm would ring before the sun rose, and I'd wake up with a mix of excitement and determination. Slipping my leotard on, I'd feel its snug embrace as if it were a uniform for a soldier preparing for battle. With sleepy eyes and a focused heart, I'd head to the gymnasium.

The gym was massive, filled with endless possibilities. The equipment stretched from wall to wall: uneven bars, beams, vaults, mats, and trampolines. It was like stepping into a wonderland where discipline was the currency for achieving the extraordinary. My training team and I worked tirelessly, and our coach pushed us to our limits. One vivid memory stands out: the end-of-session stretches.

We'd lie down on the floor, legs extended, as our coach walked through the rows, helping us improve our *spacatus* (splits). One by one, she'd press us further, stretching us beyond what felt possible. At first, it was painful—our muscles screaming in protest as she gently but firmly pressed down. But with each session, the pain lessened. Sacrifice and repetition became second nature, and eventually, I was able to do the splits in all directions—sideways, front, and even beyond a 180-degree split, like dancers move. The discomfort transformed into strength and pride, and I realized something profound: If I wanted good results, I needed to embrace sacrifice and discipline until the effort felt natural.

This lesson didn't just apply to gymnastics. It spilled over into every aspect of my life, shaping how I approached challenges, set goals, and prioritized what mattered most. Discipline wasn't just about pushing through the pain; it was about trusting the process and believing that consistent effort would yield growth.

Later, I transitioned from gymnastics to dance, carrying those same principles with me. The transition wasn't always easy, but my gymnastics training had laid a foundation of discipline that made learning new routines and styles a joy. Beyond the thrill of performing, dance reinforced what gymnastics had taught me: Progress requires effort, sacrifice, and patience.

## Understanding Discipline from a Scientific Perspective

Discipline is not just an abstract concept that we can will ourselves into; it is rooted in the way our brain functions. Our brains are wired to form habits through repeated actions, which ultimately shape our behavior and how we perceive the world. Understanding how our brain builds habits can be a powerful tool in our quest to grow spiritually and personally.

Discipline and habit formation are closely connected to the brain's basal ganglia, a small but powerful part of the brain involved in the formation of routines. The basal ganglia is the area of the brain that governs automatic behaviors—things we do without thinking. In the beginning, when we attempt a new task, such as stretching or waking up early for scripture study, the prefrontal cortex—the part of our brain responsible for decision-making and problem-solving—has to work hard to manage the new behavior. This is why these activities feel challenging at first.

However, as we repeat the behavior over and over, the brain starts to rewire itself. The effort required decreases because the brain shifts the activity from the prefrontal cortex to the basal ganglia. This transition makes the behavior more automatic and less taxing. As the saying goes, practice makes perfect—or, more accurately, practice makes automatic.

In his book *Atomic Habits*, James Clear describes this process beautifully: "Habits are the compound interest of self-improvement."[15] Each small action, repeated consistently, reinforces neural pathways in the brain. Over time, these pathways become stronger, making the behavior more natural. In the same way that financial investments compound over time, our small, daily efforts build on each other and yield significant growth in the long run.

A study published in the *European Journal of Social Psychology*[16] found that, on average, it takes sixty-six days for a new habit to become automatic. This is crucial because it shows that the key to success isn't perfection—it's consistency. The journey to developing discipline and self-control is not about executing each task flawlessly. It's about sticking with it even when you don't see immediate results. Missing a day or facing setbacks doesn't derail progress, but giving up does. This is where the two-day rule comes into play: if you miss a day, make sure you get back on track the very next day.

## The Role of Sacrifice and Patience in Building Discipline

Discipline, like anything worth achieving, requires sacrifice. In gymnastics, it was the sacrifice of sleep, free time, and comfort. It was the willingness to experience temporary pain in the pursuit of something greater. Progress would not come without commitment and effort.

---

15. James Clear, *Atomic Habits: An Easy and Proven Way to Build Good Habits and Break Bad Ones*, [New York: Avery, 2018], 16.

16. Phillippa Lally, Cornelia H. M. van Jaarsveld, Henry W. W. Potts, and Jane Wardle, "How Are Habits Formed: Modelling Habit Formation in the Real World," *European Journal of Social Psychology* 40(6), 2010, 998–1009, https://doi.org/10.1002/ejsp.674.

Spiritual growth requires the same principles. In the pursuit of becoming more Christlike, we are asked to sacrifice the natural man—our selfishness, impatience, and pride—and replace those qualities with humility, kindness, and long-suffering. This sacrifice, like the physical discomfort I experienced while training, leads to greater strength, greater spiritual resilience, and greater capacity to serve and love others.

When we build discipline in our spiritual practices, such as prayer, scripture study, and service, we must embrace the idea that spiritual growth doesn't happen overnight. Just as I had to stretch day after day to see improvement in gymnastics, spiritual disciplines require consistent effort. At times, it may feel like we are not progressing, but if we trust the process, growth will come.

Patience is key. Just as I had to wait months, even years, to achieve the flexibility I desired in gymnastics, spiritual growth can take time. But every small effort adds up. Every prayer, every moment spent in scripture study, and every act of kindness strengthens us and brings us closer to the Savior.

## Applying Discipline and Self-Control to Our Spiritual Life

As we apply these principles of discipline and self-control to our spiritual lives, it's important to recognize that the gospel is not a "one-size-fits-all" solution. Each of us has unique struggles, challenges, and goals. Some may struggle with consistency in daily prayer, while others may find it difficult to engage in scripture study or find time for service. However, the same principles of discipline and repetition can strengthen our spiritual muscles and develop a deeper connection with God.

One of the most effective ways to build spiritual discipline is through the *Come, Follow Me* program. It provides a framework for consistent study and reflection, fostering an environment of spiritual growth in our homes.

The *Come, Follow Me* program encourages small, daily efforts that compound over time, much like developing any new habit. Even on days when the scriptures seem dry or our minds wander, the practice of opening the scriptures daily builds a strong foundation of faith that will bear fruit in our lives.

## The Power of Consistency and Trust in the Process

The most important aspect of developing discipline and self-control is to trust in the process. The Lord promises that if we are consistent in our efforts to follow Him, He will provide the strength we need to overcome challenges.

Each day we choose to follow Christ is a step in the right direction. While the path may not always be easy, the consistent effort we put forth builds the spiritual discipline necessary to navigate life's challenges with grace and patience. As we trust the process, we allow the Spirit to guide us, helping us develop the discipline and self-control that will carry us through life's most difficult moments.

*Caroline Melazzo*

## Questions to Ponder

- How do you respond to challenges in your life? Do you view them as opportunities for growth or as obstacles to avoid?
- In what ways can you embrace the discomfort of the process in your own life, knowing that it leads to progress?
- What new habits have you struggled to establish? How can you apply the principle of consistency rather than perfection to those habits?
- When you face setbacks, how can you use grace to move forward rather than giving up entirely?
- What sacrifices have you made in your life to build discipline? How have these sacrifices strengthened your character?
- How can you show patience with yourself and others in the process of spiritual growth?
- How can you make scripture study a more consistent part of your daily routine?
- What is one area of your life where you can begin to develop more discipline today?

# 7

# Scripture and Goal Setting

## Using Scriptural Principles to Set and Achieve Meaningful Goals

We all set goals at different points in life. Some are small, like waking up earlier or drinking more water. While others are big, like choosing a career path, improving our faith, or making a major life decision. But if there's one thing I've learned, it's that setting goals is so much easier when we invite God into the process.

Scripture is one of the best tools we have when it comes to making real progress—not just because it gives us wisdom, but because it helps us stay focused, stay motivated, and keep an eternal perspective.

I've found that there are two powerful ways to set goals with scripture:

1. Setting a goal first and then finding scripture to support it.
2. Starting with a scripture that really speaks to us and setting a goal based on it.

No matter which way you go, scripture keeps us grounded, encouraged, and aligned with what really matters. Let's break it down.

## Setting a Goal First and Using Scripture for Support

Sometimes we already know exactly what we want to work on, but we just need strength, guidance, or a little extra push to stay on track. That's where scripture comes in. It can be a source of encouragement, motivation, and wisdom.

### Example: Cultivating Patience

Let's say someone struggles with patience, especially with family members (which, let's be honest, happens to all of us at some point). Their goal might be: Respond with kindness instead of frustration.

To help with this, they turn to James 1:19: "Wherefore, my beloved brethren, let every man be swift to hear, slow to speak, slow to wrath."

This verse becomes their anchor—a reminder that patience is a process, not just something that magically happens overnight. So, they break it down into small, doable steps:

- Short-term: Memorize James 1:19 and reflect on it daily.
- Medium-term: Pause and take a deep breath before responding to difficult situations.
- Long-term: Develop a habit of patience and kindness in conversations.

Every time they start to feel frustrated, they come back to this verse, using it as a reminder of what they're working toward and that they're not doing it alone. God is helping them.

### Example: Becoming More Disciplined in Prayer

Maybe someone wants to get better at praying consistently. They choose Alma 37:6: "By small and simple things are great things brought to pass."

This scripture reminds them that small, daily actions lead to big spiritual growth. So, they break their goal down:

- Short-term: Pray every morning and night for one week.
- Medium-term: Set aside quiet time for prayer and scripture study daily.

- Long-term: Make prayer a natural, consistent, and heartfelt part of their life.

By rooting their goal in scripture, they have something solid to hold onto when life gets busy, or distractions get in the way.

## Using Scripture as Inspiration for Goal Setting

Sometimes, instead of starting with a goal, we come across a scripture that hits us right in the heart—one that makes us stop and think. When that happens, we can use it as the foundation for setting a goal.

### Example: Moving Forward Without Seeing the Whole Path

One scripture that really stuck with me the first few times I read the Book of Mormon was 1 Nephi 4:6–7: "And I was led by the Spirit, not knowing beforehand the things which I should do. Nevertheless I went forth."

This verse always makes me stop and think. Sometimes, we feel a strong impression—whether it's about a new career, a big move, a new opportunity, or even just a simple prompting—and we have no idea how it's going to turn out.

I've had moments where I felt deep in my heart I needed to do something, even though I couldn't see the whole picture. But this scripture reminded me that it's okay not to know everything in advance. When the Spirit nudges us in a direction, we just need to take the next step and trust that everything else will fall into place.

A goal inspired by this scripture could look like this:

- Short-term: Write down any promptings or strong impressions you've had lately.
- Medium-term: Take action—apply for that program, reach out to that person, or start that project.
- Long-term: Trust that the Lord will reveal more along the way.

## Bringing It Back to Christ

No matter what kind of goal we set, we should always bring it back to Jesus Christ.

Whenever I set a goal, I like to ask myself:

- How is this helping me become more like Christ?
- What is this teaching me about Him?
- How can this goal bring me closer to Him?

### Example: Obedience and Trust Before Understanding

This is why I love Moses 5:5–6:

> And he gave commandment unto Adam, that he should offer the firstlings of their flocks for an offering unto the Lord. And Adam was obedient unto the commandments of the Lord.
>
> And after many days an angel of the Lord appeared unto Adam, saying: Why dost thou offer sacrifices unto the Lord? And Adam said unto him: I know not, save the Lord commanded me.

Adam didn't know why he was doing what he was doing—but he did it anyway. And later, God gave him understanding.

This scripture reminds me that sometimes, we feel prompted to do something, but we don't fully understand why. Maybe the Lord is asking us to serve in a way that doesn't seem to make sense yet. Maybe He's leading us to a place we didn't expect.

But if we take action in faith, like Adam, we will eventually understand.

A goal inspired by this scripture could be:

- Short-term: Act on a prompting, even if you don't fully understand it.
- Medium-term: Stay committed and trust that the purpose will become clear.
- Long-term: Reflect on how the Lord has revealed meaning and purpose in previous experiences.

And through it all, ask:

- How is this goal increasing my faith in Christ?
- How does trusting God's timing help me understand Jesus Christ's example of trust in the Father?

Because ultimately, our goals should lead us back to Him.

## Call to Action: Setting Goals with Scripture

Now it's your turn:

1. **Pick a method:** Do you already have a goal? Find a scripture to support it. Or do you have a scripture that speaks to you? Create a goal based on it.
2. **Break it into steps:** Identify short-term, medium-term, and long-term actions to achieve your goal.
3. **Write it down:** Keep your goal and scripture somewhere visible.
4. **Pray for guidance:** Ask God for wisdom, strength, and perseverance.

*Laís Gonçalves*

## Questions to Ponder

- Have you ever received a prompting to do something but didn't fully understand why? How did you act on it?
- How can scriptures like 1 Nephi 4:6–7 and Moses 5:5–6 help you trust the Lord's guidance, even when the path is unclear?
- What scripture has stood out to you lately? How could you turn it into a goal?
- How can you make sure your goals are bringing you closer to Jesus Christ?

# 8

# The Power of Gratitude

## Applying Verses on Thankfulness to Transform Your Outlook

GRATITUDE HAS THE POWER TO SHIFT OUR PERSPECTIVE, BRINGING light into even the darkest situations. It is more than just saying "thank you." It is a way of seeing life, a way of recognizing God's hand in everything. The scriptures teach us repeatedly about the power of gratitude. So many stories show that in spite of trials, when having a grateful heart, families and civilizations thrive. Paul counseled, "In everything give thanks: for this is the will of God in Christ Jesus concerning you."[17]

But how can we truly apply gratitude in our daily lives? How does thankfulness transform the way we see our trials, our blessings, and even the ordinary moments?

### A Lesson in Gratitude

I remember a time when I saw gratitude change everything. I was feeling weighed down, overwhelmed by the endless tasks demanding

17. 1 Thessalonians 5:18.

my attention. My mind was cluttered, my heart felt heavy, and my energy was drained.

My kids were in multiple activities that week, each one requiring me to drive back and forth across town for drop-offs and pick-ups. On top of that, I was managing our small remodeling company, constantly checking that we had the right materials with the right measurements at the right time, while trying to minimize waste and avoid costly mistakes.

To add to the chaos, we were in the middle of moving from one home to another. I was juggling paperwork, signatures, and last-minute details to ensure we stayed in good standing with the lending company. My head was spinning. I felt stretched thin, like I was barely holding everything together.

I knew I needed to simplify my week, so I canceled every extra commitment I could—something that's hard for me to do since my love language is serving others. But there was one thing I couldn't cancel: the final session of my 7-week, 2-hour-per-day *Healthy Relationships* course offered by Utah State University.

I rushed out the door that evening, arriving just in time. I sat down, feeling like a hurricane, my thoughts still racing with everything I had left undone. Text messages kept buzzing in about unresolved issues, and I couldn't stop thinking about my husband at home trying to put our tired kids to bed alone. I was physically present in that classroom, but my mind was somewhere else entirely.

The lesson that night was on "Building Family Strengths," and the first topic was "Stress Management."

*Well, isn't this ironic?* I thought. *This is exactly what I need right now.*

Our teacher began by asking, "How do you calm yourself down in difficult situations?"

The room filled with thoughtful responses—deep breathing, exercising, listening to music. All good answers.

Then the teacher paused and said, "Okay, now I want you all to close your eyes." I glanced around hesitantly, unsure if I could quiet my mind enough to focus. "Close your eyes," she repeated, "and I'd like you to think about all the things you are grateful for." She turned on some soft, calming music and added, "Take two minutes. Just focus on gratitude."

Maybe you can pause reading this book for a moment and do that exercise as well. Close your eyes and reflect on the things you are thankful for . . .

. . .

At first, my mind went straight to my usual list, the things I routinely thank God for in my prayers. But as the music played on, something shifted.

I began to think about things I had never consciously expressed gratitude for before:

*Wow!* I'm thankful for my arms, They helped me carry heavy wood today. I'm thankful for my legs. They allowed me to walk through the chapel walls earlier. I'm thankful for my eyes. They help me see so many beautiful colors!

My thoughts kept flowing, faster and faster, my heart filling with gratitude for things I had taken for granted. The more I reflected, the more I realized just how abundantly blessed I was.

When the music stopped, I didn't want the moment to end. *I needed more time.*

I opened my eyes, and something was different. My heart was full, and my shoulders felt lighter. The overwhelming stress I felt just moments before loosened its grip on me. I still had a full to-do list waiting for me, but somehow, it didn't feel as heavy anymore.

Gratitude didn't change my circumstances. It changed *me*.

At first, my mind had been consumed by what I lacked, unfinished tasks, unresolved issues, and countless things I couldn't control. I had been asking God for solutions, for things to improve, for my burdens to be lifted.

But that simple two-minute exercise shifted my heart. Instead of asking, I began thanking Him—not just for the blessings I hoped for, but for the blessings I already had.

And that's when everything began to change.

In the days that followed, I realized that the outcome of all that stress brought with it unexpected blessings. I was able to see things I might have missed before, like how capable my husband was at managing bedtime routines when I couldn't be there. Or how my kids didn't need everything to be perfect; they just needed me to be present, loving, and willing to laugh with them at the end of a long day.

Gratitude didn't erase my busy schedule, but it transformed my outlook. My heart was lighter, my mind was clearer, and my burdens no longer felt impossible to carry.

I realized that when we take time to focus on what we have, even in the middle of overwhelming circumstances, our perspective changes. Gratitude turns frustration into peace. It doesn't fix everything, but it does help us remember that God's hand is always in our lives, even in the messiest moments.

## Gratitude in the Gospel: A Commandment and a Blessing

Gratitude is not just a nice thought. It is a commandment and a principle with real power. The Lord told us, "Thou shalt thank the Lord thy God in all things."[18] Not just in the good times. Not just when things go our way. But in all things.

Jesus Himself showed us the ultimate example of gratitude—not just in abundance, but in the face of unimaginable suffering. At the Last Supper, knowing He was about to endure Gethsemane and the cross, "He took the cup, and gave thanks."[19] In that sacred moment, Jesus chose gratitude, demonstrating that even in our darkest hours, we can turn to the Father with a thankful heart.

How often do we do the opposite? We see the missing pieces, the unfinished parts of our lives, the unanswered prayers, the things we still long for. But when we choose to focus on what we *do* have and give thanks, even before things change, we invite miracles.

The scriptures are filled with promises to those who live in thankfulness. The prophet Alma, counseled, "Let thy heart be full of thanks unto God; and if ye do these things, ye shall be lifted up at the last day."[20] And the Lord Himself revealed, "He who receiveth all things with thankfulness shall be made glorious; and the things of this earth shall be added unto him, even a hundred fold, yea, more."[21]

---

18. Doctrine and Covenants 59:7.

19. Matthew 26:27.

20. Alma 37:37.

21. Doctrine and Covenants 78:19.

## The Everyday Practice of Gratitude

Gratitude is not just something we feel—but it is something we practice. It is a habit, a way of thinking, and a way of speaking. Elder David A. Bednar taught: "The most meaningful and spiritual prayers I have experienced contained many expressions of thanks and few, if any, requests."[22]

I've found this to be true in my own life. While I've had powerful experiences fasting for things I deeply desired or needed, my most meaningful fasts have been those offered purely in gratitude. Something changes when I fast with no other motive than to thank the Lord. My heart feels fuller, my mind clearer, and I walk away feeling closer to Him; not because my circumstances have changed, but because my perspective has.

How would our lives change if we made gratitude our default response? If, instead of complaining about what isn't, we praised God for what is? Here are some ways to practice gratitude daily:

1. **Start with Prayer**—Make gratitude the center of your conversations with God. Spend a whole prayer just giving thanks.
2. **Write it Down**—Keep a gratitude journal, recording things big and small that you are grateful for.
3. **Speak Gratitude**—Express thanks to those around you, and let them know how they have blessed your life.
4. **Find Gratitude in Challenges**—Even in trials, ask yourself: *What is God teaching me through this?*

## Finding Gratitude in Disappointment

There are moments in life when gratitude feels natural, when things go our way, when blessings are easy to recognize, and when prayers are answered exactly as we hoped. But there are also moments when gratitude feels impossible, when our hearts ache, when prayers seem unanswered, and when disappointment weighs heavily on us.

I experienced this when my mother passed away.

---

22. David A. Bednar, *Pray Always*, General Conference (Salt Lake City: The Church of Jesus Christ of Latter-day Saints), October 2008, Gospel Library App.

During her final weeks, my dad's words echoed repeatedly in our home:

"What does the Lord want me to learn from this?"

"What is the lesson here?"

"Why are we going through this?"

Those questions shaped how we faced our grief. My dad's example of faith turned what could have been overwhelming sorrow into something sacred. Instead of feeling consumed by loss, we began to look for what God was teaching us.

I remember feeling that if the Lord had allowed us to have my mother for only twenty-one years of my life, then there must have been something far greater for her to do in heaven and something important for us to learn here. Rather than dwelling on what I was losing, I began to focus on what I had been given.

I thought about the incredible lessons I had learned from her, her love of service, her strength, and her faith. I reflected on the many moments we had shared, the conversations, the laughter, and the memories that had shaped me. Gratitude filled my heart, not just for what she had been to me, but for the time God had allowed me to have with her.

That perspective didn't mean I wasn't heartbroken. I was. And until her very last day, I believed with all my heart that God would heal her. I *knew* He could. I had prayed with faith, certain that a miracle would come. When things didn't unfold the way I had hoped, I felt almost numb, like I couldn't quite grasp that this was really happening.

But even then, I felt peace. As I stood at her funeral, surrounded by family and friends, I wasn't overwhelmed by grief. I was overwhelmed by gratitude. I had spent the days leading up to it gathering pictures of her, from her childhood through her 50s, and displayed them on a board for everyone to see. As I looked at those photos, I realized something powerful. *She had lived a full life, a life of love, of service, and of joy.*

I knew in my heart that her story wasn't over. I knew she had important work to do beyond this life, and that we would be together again. My gratitude for that knowledge softened the pain of her passing and filled me with hope.

That experience taught me something I will never forget: Gratitude doesn't mean ignoring our struggles or pretending everything is easy.

It means trusting that God is still writing our story. His plan is still unfolding, even when we can't yet see the ending.

And with that realization, my heart softened. Instead of frustration, I felt peace. Instead of resentment, I felt joy. I saw what was already in my hands instead of what I thought was missing.

*Letícia Araujo*

## Questions to Ponder

If there's one thing I know, it's this: Gratitude changes everything. It shifts your focus, strengthens your faith, and invites miracles into your life. If you're feeling overwhelmed, discouraged, or stuck in a season of waiting, I invite you to consider these questions:

- When was the last time you paused to truly thank God for what you already have?
- How has gratitude helped you find peace during challenging times?
- What simple habit can you develop to make gratitude a more central part of your daily life?

Try this:

1. Take a moment to list 10 things you are grateful for—right now.
2. Spend your next prayer only expressing gratitude—no requests.
3. Find a scripture on gratitude and write it somewhere you will see it daily.

As you do this, watch how your outlook changes. Watch how you begin to see God's hand in places you never noticed before.

Gratitude doesn't change your circumstances. It changes *you*. And that changes everything.

# Part III

# Relationships and Community

# 9

# Loving Your Neighbor

## Practical Acts of Kindness and Service Inspired by Scripture

LOVING OUR NEIGHBOR IS MORE THAN JUST A KIND THOUGHT. IT'S AN active, intentional way of living. The Savior taught: "By this shall all men know that ye are my disciples, if ye have love one to another."[23]

Love isn't always convenient or easy, but it's often in those challenging moments that the greatest blessings unfold.

I often think I'm the worst at recognizing others' needs, especially when I'm not close to them. I love to serve, and if there's something to be done, I'll leave everything behind to do it. But I feel it's hard to know the right thing to do—and the feeling that I could be doing a better job at easing someone else's burdens never quite leaves. But I'm learning that grace fills the gaps where my efforts fall short, and that God doesn't ask for perfection—only a willing heart.

Despite my personal doubts, I've been incredibly blessed by angels who have been examples in my life, and have shown me what true ministering looks like by ministering the way the Savior did.

23. John 13:35.

When I was pregnant with my first child in Rexburg, Idaho, I was assigned two ministering sisters in my English-speaking ward. One of them, to my surprise, was from my home country, who had just moved into the ward. I already knew several sisters in the ward, but I had never met this new, kind friend, Simone. And yet, she immediately went above and beyond to make me feel loved.

The first thing she did was organize a baby shower for me. I remember thinking: *Wow! We barely know each other!* She visited me and often checked in to see if I needed anything. Having her as a friend and ministering sister felt like having a piece of home. She was exactly what I needed at that moment. Even though I had other friends in town, she ministered to me in such a motherly way that I felt the Lord had sent her to fill the gap I had since my own mother passed four years prior.

I had another experience, years later, when we were living in Lehi, Utah. I was pregnant with my second child, Isabella. Just before she was born, we decided to move to a new ward—this time a Portuguese-speaking ward in our boundary. We made the change because we felt our son would better understand the gospel in Portuguese. But again, God had plans I hadn't foreseen.

I had made wonderful friends in our previous ward, and even though I left the ward, they still kept me on their "meal calendar" for when the baby came. To my surprise, the new ward also added us to their calendar. We were blessed with two to three weeks of meals delivered to our home from families in both wards.

I felt carried by the Savior through the kindness of friends. Their simple acts of service lifted my burdens and allowed me to focus on healing and bonding with my children. Even though family members came to help with both babies, nothing could fully replace my own mother's presence—but the love shown by these sisters came close. They were being true disciples.

Some of these friends became like family. They love my children like their own nieces and nephews. That kind of love is one of the most precious gifts a parent can receive—to know that others care deeply for your children.

Those acts of kindness, though simple, reflected something deeply sacred. I felt held. I felt seen. I felt loved.

## The Hidden Blessings in Service

Not every experience of serving others is as easy as sending a meal when it is needed. At times, we need to tune our spirits to the Lord's frequency, so we can recognize the promptings to be an instrument in His hands. And when we do, the Savior taught: "Whosoever shall give to drink unto one of these little ones a cup of cold water . . . verily I say unto you, he shall in no wise lose his reward."[24]

Despite sometimes not knowing exactly what to do for someone, the simple act of showing love can be enough. And the more we act on those promptings, the more God trusts us to follow them—so He sends more. These moments shape us. They show us what it means to "mourn with those that mourn and comfort those that stand in need of comfort."[25]

I've realized that loving our neighbor doesn't always look like a grand gesture. Sometimes it's simply sharing what we have, even when it requires sacrifice.

We may never know how far a simple act of kindness can reach. But when we love and serve as He would, we become instruments in His hands, and we find ourselves blessed in ways we couldn't have foreseen.

## Living the Principle of Loving Your Neighbor

If there's one thing I've learned, it's that God often places people in our path who need exactly what we can offer—even when we don't feel ready or capable.

Here are some practical ways we can love our neighbors as the Savior taught:

- **Be Available:** Sometimes the greatest gift you can give is your time. Pause to listen. Offer a ride. Reach out to someone who seems lonely.
- **Be Generous with What You Have:** Whether it's a meal, a guest room, or a simple word of encouragement, share what you can. Even small things make a difference.

24. Matthew 10:42.

25. Mosiah 18:9.

- **Follow Promptings:** If you feel a nudge to call someone, visit a friend, or offer help—act on it. Those quiet whispers are often invitations to bless someone's life.
- **See the Person, Not the Burden:** Loving your neighbor may require stepping out of your comfort zone. Focus on the person—their story, their needs—and trust that God will make your efforts enough.

"When ye are in the service of your fellow beings ye are only in the service of your God."[26]

## Becoming an Instrument in God's Hands

These experiences have shown me that God's blessings are often hidden in the quiet moments of love and service—the baby showers, the warm meals, the loving text messages, the quiet hugs.

When we act with love, we are never left empty. The more we give, the more we gain. It's not always in material ways, but in meaningful connections, peace of mind, and a deeper understanding of Christ's love.

If the Lord gives us more—whether it's time, resources, or opportunities—it's because He trusts us to use those blessings to lift others.

Loving your neighbor is one of the most powerful ways to follow Jesus Christ. It calls for more than good intentions; it calls for action.

*Letícia Araújo*

## Questions to Ponder

- Who in your life might need your kindness today?
- What is one way you can serve someone this week that will brighten their day?
- How has showing love and compassion strengthened your relationship with God and others?

26. Mosiah 2:17.

Consider this challenge:

- Pray for someone who may be feeling alone or burdened. Ask the Lord how you can help them.
- Perform a small act of kindness this week—a note, a visit, a text—that reminds someone they are loved.
- Reflect on how serving others brings you closer to Christ.

As we follow His example, we will find our hearts softened, our relationships strengthened, and our capacity to love increased.

# 10

# Conflict Resolution in Light of Scripture

## Approaching Forgiveness and Reconciliation Through Biblical Teachings

Let's be real—conflict is just part of being human. Whether it's a family argument, tension in a group chat, or a full-blown disagreement at church, we all deal with it. People have different opinions, emotions run high, and sometimes, we flat-out misunderstand each other. But as followers of Christ, we're called to handle these situations with love, patience, and a desire to build bridges, not burn them.

Jesus was pretty clear about this one:

- Matthew 5:9: "Blessed are the peacemakers: for they shall be called the children of God."
- Doctrine and Covenants 64:8–9: "My disciples, in days of old, sought occasion against one another and forgave not one another in their hearts; and for this evil they were afflicted

and sorely chastened. Wherefore, I say unto you, that ye ought to forgive one another."

- 3 Nephi 11:29: "For verily, verily I say unto you, he that hath the spirit of contention is not of me, but is of the devil."

Elder Jeffrey R. Holland, in his talk *The Ministry of Reconciliation*, emphasizes the importance of peacemaking in today's world:

> Jesus is asking us to be instruments of His grace—to be 'ambassadors for Christ' in 'the ministry of reconciliation,' as Paul described it to the Corinthians. The Healer of every wound, He who rights every wrong, asks us to labor with Him in the daunting task of peacemaking in a world that won't find it any other way.[27]

Translation? Being a peacemaker isn't just about keeping quiet when things get messy. It's an active pursuit of harmony through Christlike attributes. However, being a peacemaker does not mean tolerating abuse or allowing ourselves to be mistreated repeatedly. The Lord expects us to set healthy boundaries while still maintaining a forgiving heart.

Forgiveness is central to resolving conflict and one of the toughest things we're asked to do. Holding grudges feels *so* much easier sometimes. But Christ set the example.

## Christ's Example of Forgiveness

- Luke 23:34: "Then said Jesus, Father, forgive them; for they know not what they do."
- Mosiah 26:30: "Yea, and as often as my people repent will I forgive them their trespasses against me."

President Gordon B. Hinckley once taught: "The willingness to forgive is a sign of spiritual maturity. It is one of the great virtues to which we all should aspire."[28]

---

27. Jeffrey R. Holland, *The Ministry of Reconciliation*, General Conference (Salt Lake City: The Church of Jesus Christ of Latter-day Saints), October 2018, Gospel Library App.

28. Gordon B. Hinckley, *Standing For Something: 10 Neglected Virtues That Will Heal Our Hearts and Homes*, [New York: Three Rivers Press, 2001].

James R. Rasband, in his address *Faith to Forgive Grievous Harms: Accepting the Atonement as Restitution*, discusses the profound connection between forgiveness and the Atonement: "Our salvation is conditioned on forgiving others because when we refuse to forgive, what we are really saying is that we reject, or don't quite trust, the Atonement."[29]

Oof. That one stings.

I recall a time when I struggled to forgive someone important in my life who had wronged me. The weight of resentment grew heavier each day, each month, and each year. Holding onto that started to change me. I became bitter. I lost hope and faith in that person and in myself. I started to ask God how this person could do that to me. This turned into thinking about how God could allow this to happen. My thoughts started to become dangerous. I soon started questioning my beliefs, the way I was raised, and ultimately the restored gospel.

My pain cracked open the door for all sorts of thoughts that weren't coming from a good place. And honestly? That's *exactly* what Satan wanted. He didn't care about my anger toward this person; he wanted me to turn that anger toward the gospel. He wanted me *stuck* in that bitterness. He wanted me to be miserable in my anger. Miserable, just like he is.

I can't pinpoint exactly when I started to let go of these distorted beliefs, but I remember thinking, *Wow, this isn't healthy, and it doesn't feel right to blame everything on the church.* I think that's when I started to turn more to Heavenly Father and plead for Him to remove these feelings from me. It was already hard enough to feel so much anger toward this person, I couldn't bear to start hating the Church too. I needed the Church. I needed the gospel. I needed my Savior.

Am I 100 percent over it? Nope. But I'm *on the path* to forgiveness. And that's enough for now. With this being said, there is a distinction between forgiveness and reconciliation. While the Lord commands us to forgive, reconciliation is not always necessary or possible—especially in cases of abuse or harm. We can forgive without allowing ourselves to be continually hurt.

---

29. James R. Rasband, *Faith to Forgive Grievous Harms: Accepting the Atonement as Restitution,* BYU Devotional, October 23rd, 2012, https://speeches.byu.edu/talks/james-r-rasband/faith-to-forgive-grievous-harms-atonement-restitution/.

Let's make one thing very clear: Forgiving someone does *not* mean you have to let them back into your life. There's a huge difference between forgiveness and reconciliation.

The Savior calls us to forgive, but He also desires for us to be safe and protected. Abuse—whether physical, emotional, sexual, or spiritual—is never condoned by God, and those who experience it are not obligated to reconcile with their abuser in order to be at peace with the Lord.

Doctrine and Covenants 64:10: "I, the Lord, will forgive whom I will forgive, but of you it is required to forgive all men."

Forgiveness, in the context of abuse, is about personal healing. It does not excuse the actions of the abuser nor requires the victim to engage with them again. Instead, it means releasing the burden of anger and hurt so that it does not continue to damage one's well-being.

Some relationships are better left behind, and that's okay.

## The Process of Reconciliation

If reconciliation is possible, it requires humility, open communication, and a willingness to mend relationships.

The following principles help guide reconciliation and healing:

1. **Practice Active Listening**—Proverbs 18:13: "He that answereth a matter before he heareth it, it is folly and shame unto him."

Instead of mentally preparing your response while someone speaks, focus on truly hearing them. This prevents misunderstandings and shows respect.

Example: A married couple struggling with communication may find that setting aside time to listen—without interrupting or jumping to conclusions—helps both partners feel heard and valued, ultimately strengthening their relationship.

2. **Extend Kindness and Understanding**—Ephesians 4:32: "And be ye kind one to another, tenderhearted, forgiving one another, even as God for Christ's sake hath forgiven you."

Kindness is not weakness. Choosing to approach conflict with gentleness often leads to better resolutions.

Example: In the workplace, a manager who approaches a frustrated employee with patience rather than defensiveness may find that the employee is more willing to engage in a productive conversation, reducing workplace tension and increasing morale.

3. **Seek Reconciliation, Not Just an Apology**—Matthew 5:23–24: "First be reconciled to thy brother, and then come and offer thy gift."

A true resolution involves understanding and change, not just words. Focus on finding solutions rather than assigning blame.

Example: Two friends who have drifted apart due to a misunderstanding may work toward reconciliation by discussing the root of the issue and making efforts to rebuild trust, rather than simply exchanging a superficial apology.

4. **Turn to the Lord in Prayer**—Alma 34:19: "Yea, humble yourselves, and continue in prayer unto him."

Prayer softens hearts and brings divine guidance in resolving conflicts. Seeking the Lord's help often opens doors to peace that seemed impossible.

Example: A family experiencing long-standing discord may come together in prayer, seeking guidance and strength to forgive past grievances, leading to healing and restoration over time.

Elder Dieter F. Uchtdorf taught:

> Brothers and sisters, there is enough heartache and sorrow in this life without our adding to it through our own stubbornness, bitterness, and resentment.
>
> We are not perfect.
>
> The people around us are not perfect. People do things that annoy, disappoint, and anger. In this mortal life it will always be that way.
>
> Nevertheless, we must let go of our grievances. Part of the purpose of mortality is to learn how to let go of such things. *That is the Lord's way.*
>
> Remember, heaven is filled with those who have this in common: They are forgiven. And they forgive.

> Lay your burden at the Savior's feet. Let go of judgment. Allow Christ's Atonement to change and heal your heart. Love one another. Forgive one another.
>
> The merciful will obtain mercy.[30]

At the end of the day, life's too short to stay angry. Conflict is going to happen, but how we handle it is what defines our spiritual growth. So take a deep breath, set some boundaries, and start the journey toward peace. You've got this.

*Ana de Castro*

## Questions to Ponder

- Are there any unresolved conflicts in my life that I need to address?
- Have I truly forgiven those who have wronged me, or am I still holding onto resentment?
- Am I maintaining relationships that are harmful to my emotional or spiritual well-being?
- What boundaries do I need to establish to protect my peace while still living in a Christlike manner?
- How can I ensure that my communication is clear, kind, and firm when setting boundaries?
- Have I sought divine guidance in my efforts to forgive and move forward?
- What role does personal accountability play in my relationships, and how can I improve?
- How can I distinguish between necessary distance and avoidance rooted in fear or anger?
- What Christlike attributes can I develop to handle conflicts with wisdom and compassion?
- Am I creating an environment where others feel respected, even when boundaries need to be enforced?

---

30. Dieter F. Uchtdorf, *The Merciful Obtain Mercy*, General Conference (Salt Lake City: The Church of Jesus Christ of Latter-day Saints), April 2012, Gospel Library App.

# 11

# Building a Strong Family Foundation

## Principles for Nurturing Love and Respect in Family Life

CREATING A STRONG FAMILY FOUNDATION IS NOT ABOUT HAVING A perfect past. It's about choosing today to build something better. Whether you're starting with a legacy of love or trying to change the course of your family's history, it's never too late to begin. My mother's story is a powerful reminder that no matter how broken a family may feel, through faith and effort, it is possible to rebuild and create a home centered on Christ.

My mother was baptized at the age of fourteen in Guarulhos, São Paulo, Brazil. She grew up in a humble home as the third of six children, surrounded by challenges. Both of her parents smoked, and my grandfather struggled with alcohol addiction, often coming home late at night, bruised and stumbling. One of her most vivid memories was being asked by my grandfather to light his *cachimbo* (pipe). She hated that task, and as she smelled the tobacco smoke, she made a promise to herself: When she grew up, she would never smoke.

Despite these challenges, my mother's heart was always searching for something better. She witnessed firsthand the consequences of addiction and the toll it took on her family. The promise to herself to never smoke was more than a simple vow; it was a deep, almost unconscious desire to escape the cycle of addiction that had plagued her family for generations. She yearned for something greater, something that would help her overcome these trials and provide her with the strength to live a better life.

When the missionaries taught her family the gospel, it was the Word of Wisdom that captured her heart. She saw it not only as a health code but as an answer to her unspoken prayers, a way to break the cycle of addiction and create a new story. At just fourteen years old, she chose to be baptized, knowing the gospel could give her the tools to build a stronger, happier future. This was a turning point in her life, as she recognized that the gospel was the foundation she needed to help her and her family break free from the past.

Her life wasn't perfect, and our family faced its own challenges. However, my mother's faith never wavered, and she chose to build her family on the foundation of Jesus Christ. She demonstrated this through her actions, teaching us that when Christ is the center of our lives, everything else begins to align. No matter what difficulties arose, she never gave up on us or on the principles of the gospel. Her determination to prioritize faith and family reminds me of the scripture in Helaman 5:12:

> And now, my sons, remember, remember that it is upon the rock of our Redeemer, who is Christ, the Son of God, that ye must build your foundation; that when the devil shall send forth his mighty winds, yea, his shafts in the whirlwind, yea, when all his hail and his mighty storm shall beat upon you, it shall have no power over you to drag you down to the gulf of misery and endless wo, because of the rock upon which ye are built, which is a sure foundation.

## The Key: Never Give Up on Family

One of the greatest lessons I've learned from my mother's life is that we should never give up on our families, no matter how broken they may seem. Families are God's plan for us, and while they are often messy and imperfect, they are also the place where we experience the greatest joy and growth. The gospel teaches us that families are essential to God's plan of salvation, and it is through our families that we are given the opportunity to learn, grow, and become more like Christ.

In my own life, there were times when I wondered how we could possibly overcome some of the challenges we faced as a family. Yet, as I reflect on my mother's example, I realize that even in our hardest moments, we could always rely on the strength of the Savior. We learned that despite life's trials, if we continue to focus on what is good, what is eternal, and what is centered in Christ, we can find peace, hope, and healing.

My mother prioritized the basics of gospel living: family prayer, scripture study, and quality time. Every night, we gathered around my parents' bed to kneel in prayer. These moments weren't always perfect. We were sometimes tired, distracted, or even impatient, but the act of gathering together in prayer united us. It reminded us of God's presence and helped us feel His peace, especially after a long day. Prayer brought our family closer together, creating a sense of unity that couldn't be broken by anything in the world.

Family scripture study followed a similar pattern. Even if we only read a few verses, my mother made sure we opened the scriptures together. Sometimes, we didn't fully understand what we read, but the practice of consistently reading together created a foundation of faith in our home. President Russell M. Nelson emphasized the importance of this practice, saying, "Frequent participation in temple service and regular family scripture study nourish a marriage and strengthen faith within a family."[31] These moments were not always easy, but they created a culture of faith in our home.

## Practical Practices for Strong Families

One of the most meaningful traditions I've carried into my own family life is a simple practice we call "highs and lows." During dinner, each family member takes turns sharing their high point of the

---

31. Russell M. Nelson, *Nurturing Marriage*, General Conference (Salt Lake City: The Church of Jesus Christ of Latter-day Saints), April 2006, Gospel Library App.

day (or week, if it's Sunday), something that was difficult or challenging (a low), and something they're grateful for. This tradition fosters connection, empathy, and gratitude, helping us to focus on the good while acknowledging life's challenges.

As President Henry B. Eyring taught, "I felt more gratitude for the softening and refining that come because of the Atonement of the Savior Jesus Christ."[32] Gratitude is not just a way to express thanks, but it is a practice that refines our hearts. When we acknowledge the blessings we've received, both big and small, we cultivate a spirit of humility and love. This simple act of sharing builds love and understanding within the family, strengthening bonds and deepening our connection with one another.

Another practice that has been invaluable in my own family is taking time to celebrate small successes. Whether it is a school achievement, a personal victory, or even an effort to serve one another, recognizing and celebrating these moments helps to build confidence and unity in the home. Celebrating successes, no matter how small, creates a positive environment where family members feel valued and loved.

## Family Foundations: The Basics

Elder David A. Bednar taught, "We can become more diligent and concerned at home as we express love—and consistently show it."[33] Small, consistent practices like family prayer, scripture study, and quality time form the bedrock of strong families. These small, seemingly simple acts lay the foundation for deeper connection and spiritual growth.

- **Family Prayer:** Kneeling together in prayer reminds us that we are united, not just with each other but with God. Prayer is an intimate conversation with our Heavenly Father that brings us closer to Him and to one another. These moments of prayer

32. Henry B. Eyring, *O Remember, Remember*, General Conference (Salt Lake City: The Church of Jesus Christ of Latter-day Saints), October 2007, Gospel Library App.
33. David A. Bednar, *More Diligent and Concerned at Home*, General Conference (Salt Lake City: The Church of Jesus Christ of Latter-day Saints), October 2009, Gospel Library App.

invite the Spirit into our homes and give us the strength to face life's challenges with faith.

- **Family Scripture Study:** Sharing the scriptures as a family allows us to learn and grow together. In our family, scripture study wasn't always perfect. We sometimes read only a few verses or spent more time discussing questions than reading. But by making scripture study a consistent practice, we learned to apply gospel principles to our lives, strengthening our faith and helping us navigate challenges with God's guidance.
- **Quality Time:** My mother understood the importance of spending meaningful time together. Whether it was celebrating small achievements or simply talking, these moments of connection made a lasting impact. Quality time helps to build trust and understanding between family members, fostering a deeper sense of love and unity.

## Meeting Individual Needs

Every family member is unique, and understanding these differences is key to building a strong foundation. Gary Chapman's *The Five Love Languages* teaches that people express and receive love in different ways. These include words of affirmation, quality time, acts of service, physical touch, or receiving gifts.

By recognizing and honoring each family member's love language, we can create deeper emotional connections. For instance, a child who thrives on words of affirmation might benefit from daily encouragement, while another might feel most loved through shared activities. Understanding these differences allows us to respond to one another's needs with empathy and love, creating a more harmonious family environment.

## Boundaries and Respect

Strong families are built on love, but love also requires boundaries. Dr. Henry Cloud and Dr. John Townsend, in their book *Boundaries*, explain, "boundaries are essential for defining who you are and what responsibilities you hold."[34] Healthy boundaries teach accountability, respect, and kindness.

My mother modeled this by setting clear expectations for behavior while always leading with love. She taught us the importance of respecting one another's personal space, feelings, and opinions. She helped us learn to resolve conflicts with patience and forgiveness, creating a home where discipline and respect went hand in hand. Boundaries are not meant to limit love; rather, they protect and strengthen it by teaching us how to live harmoniously with one another.

Some of our most sacred family memories have taken place within the walls of the temple. There is something profoundly powerful about being in the house of the Lord together, united not just by earthly ties but by eternal covenants and purpose.

One of the most unforgettable experiences we've had as a family was performing baptisms for the dead. On that day, I witnessed my son step into the baptismal font—not just as my child, but as a worthy priesthood holder acting in the service of the Lord. With reverence and love, he baptized me on behalf of one of our ancestors. Then, one by one, he baptized his own siblings while my husband stood nearby to perform the confirmations. It was one of those moments that feels like heaven and earth are meeting in the same room.

There was no need for grand speeches or pictures. The Spirit did all the teaching. In that quiet, holy space, our family was reminded of the eternal nature of our relationships and the sacred responsibilities we share. The temple was no longer just a place—it became a symbol of who we are becoming as a family.

Temple attendance isn't always easy. Between busy schedules, school, church callings, and the everyday demands of life, it often requires planning, sacrifice, and commitment. But I have learned that there is no greater investment we can make in our family than helping each other feel the Spirit and understand the bigger picture of eternity.

Even when our children are young, we can take them to walk the temple grounds, share family history stories, and talk about what it

---

34. Dr. Henry Cloud and Dr. John Townsend, *Boundaries: When to Say Yes, How to Say No to Take Control of Your Life.* [Peabody: Christian Book, 1992].

means to make and keep covenants. These small moments, over time, plant seeds of testimony that will grow into deep spiritual roots.

Family temple attendance reminds us that we belong to something bigger than ourselves. It teaches us reverence, unity, purpose, and love. And more than anything, it strengthens our resolve to live in such a way that one day, we can be together forever—not just in word or hope, but in truth.

## Practical Steps to Build a Strong Family Foundation

Here are some practical steps to nurture love and respect in your family:

- **Never Give Up on Your Family:** Even if your family feels broken, there is always hope. Make the decision to focus on what you can build today.
- **Prioritize Family Prayer and Scripture Study:** Set aside time each day to kneel in prayer and study scriptures together. These practices invite the Spirit and strengthen family bonds.
- **Start a Gratitude Tradition:** Implement a "highs and lows" tradition at meals or during family time. Sharing highlights, challenges, and moments of gratitude fosters connection and understanding.
- **Learn and Apply Love Languages:** Understand the unique love languages of your family members and make an effort to meet their needs.
- **Set Boundaries with Love:** Establish clear expectations and enforce them with kindness. Healthy boundaries create safety and respect.
- **Celebrate Successes:** Acknowledge and celebrate even the smallest victories as a family. Gratitude strengthens relationships and brings joy.
- **Attend the Temple as a Family**: Regular temple attendance—when possible as a couple, with older children, or even as individuals—reminds the family of eternal goals and sacred covenants. Visiting the temple grounds, doing family history together, or planning trips to perform baptisms for

ancestors can instill a sense of peace, purpose, and connection to God and each other.

## A Family Built on Christ

Building a family on the foundation of Jesus Christ is the greatest gift we can give to ourselves and our posterity. As Helaman 5:12 teaches, Christ is the "sure foundation" that withstands life's storms.

No matter where your family is today, it's never too late to start building—or rebuilding. Small, consistent efforts, combined with faith in Jesus Christ, can transform any home into a haven of love, respect, and joy.

As the hymn "Love at Home" so beautifully reminds us: "There is beauty all around, when there's love at home."[35]

When we build our families on Christ, we create a home where love, respect, and joy can thrive. It's not about perfection, but about choosing every day to nurture our relationships and strengthen our faith. Let's strive to create homes filled with love, where Christ is the cornerstone and joy abounds.

*Caroline Melazzo*

## Questions to Ponder

- What are the challenges your family has faced, and how has your faith helped you overcome them?
- How can you ensure that Christ remains the center of your family life?
- What small, consistent practices can you implement in your family to strengthen your spiritual foundation?
- How can understanding each family member's love language improve the relationships in your home?
- In what ways can you set healthy boundaries with love to ensure a respectful environment in your home?
- How does the act of expressing gratitude help build stronger connections within your family?

---

35. "Love at Home," *Hymns*, No. 294, [Salt Lake City: The Church of Jesus Christ of Latter-day Saints, 1985].

- What can you do today to start rebuilding or strengthening the foundation of your family?
- How can you celebrate small victories in your family life to encourage growth and gratitude?

# 12
# Creating a Faith-Based Community

## Encouraging Unity and Mutual Growth Through Scripture

### The Power of Friendships in Our Faith Journey

Friends play a significant role in our lives. They shape our thoughts, influence our aspirations, and help us become who we are meant to be. Some friendships uplift and inspire us, while others can lead us in directions we never intended to go.

I've always been an outgoing, spontaneous person, someone who loves meeting new people and getting to know their stories. I have always been fascinated by what makes people who they are, where they come from, their family values, their dreams, and even their beliefs.

For me, friendships have never been about just having fun or fitting in. They have always been about connection, growth, and learning from one another. I believe that when we bring faith into our friendships, we create something truly powerful—a community that lifts and strengthens each other, that learns together, and that grows in Christ.

## A Transformational Year in Jackson Hole, Wyoming

In 2008, I had the life-changing opportunity to be an exchange student in Jackson Hole, Wyoming. I was excited, but I was also stepping into the unknown—a new country, a new culture, and a new language.

At first, I felt like I wasn't truly myself. I couldn't communicate the way I wanted to. I had so much to say, but the words didn't always come out the way I intended. It was frustrating because I wanted people to know who I really was—what I cared about, what I believed in—but the language barrier made me feel stuck.

For someone who had always been social and confident, this was a humbling experience. But I had always been a positive person, so I knew that this was just a season, a challenge to be embraced.

What I didn't expect was how much this experience would strengthen my faith.

In moments when I felt different or lonely, when I felt like no one around me could fully understand what I was going through, I turned to my Heavenly Father.

During that year, I developed a deep love for scripture study, particularly the Doctrine and Covenants. I read passages on my own, seeking guidance and comfort. In doing so, I found a stronger connection to my Savior.

I started to realize that Jesus Christ understood me perfectly—even when no one else did.

## The Blessings of a Loving Host Family

A major part of my experience in Jackson Hole was my host family. They were incredibly loving and patient with me.

They did more than just provide a home. They opened their hearts to me.

- They helped me improve my English, gently correcting me and helping me express myself more clearly

- They encouraged my growth, making me feel like I truly belonged
- They shared their family traditions and culture with me, teaching me lessons that would stay with me for life

Their kindness made all the difference. They gave me a safe space to grow, learn, and embrace this new chapter.

Even before I could see it, God had placed me exactly where I needed to be—surrounded by people who would shape my journey and draw me closer to Him.

## Discovering a Larger Purpose

Before my exchange experience, my world was smaller, centered around my home country, my friends, and my familiar surroundings. Jackson Hole changed that.

It was there that I realized the gospel is for everyone.

I had always known this in theory, but experiencing it firsthand made it real.

I met people from different backgrounds and walks of life, yet I saw a common need: Everyone was searching for something greater. Everyone was seeking Christ, whether they realized it or not.

And so, even in moments of self-doubt, when I felt nervous about my English or unsure about how to express myself, I still shared the gospel.

I talked about my faith with my new friends. I shared my testimony in simple ways. And to my surprise, some of them wanted to know more.

Some of them even met with the missionaries.

It was a profound realization. This world is full of people thirsting for the truth. And when we have the truth, it is our privilege to share it.

## Building a Faith-Based Community Starts with Us

Creating a faith-based community begins with each of us. By embodying the teachings of Jesus Christ, we become positive influences in the lives of others. This doesn't mean our lives are free from trials or that we experience happiness every day. In fact, it's through our challenges we demonstrate the strength and comfort faith provides. By leaning on Jesus Christ during difficult times, we not only better ourselves, but also show others the power of His support.

The scriptures emphasize the importance of unity and mutual growth. In Romans 14:19, we are encouraged to "let us therefore follow after the things which make for peace, and things wherewith one may edify another."

Similarly, Ephesians 4:2–3 advises us: "With all lowliness and meekness, with longsuffering, forbearing one another in love; Endeavouring to keep the unity of the Spirit in the bond of peace."

These passages remind us that fostering unity requires intentional effort, patience, and love. We are not meant to journey through life alone. Our faith is meant to be shared, and our relationships are meant to uplift one another.

## Building Bridges Instead of Walls

President Russell M. Nelson spoke about the importance of building connections rather than divisions. He stated: "Ultimately, we realize that only the comprehension of the true Fatherhood of God can bring full appreciation of the true brotherhood of men and the true sisterhood of women. That understanding inspires us with passionate desire to build bridges of cooperation instead of walls of segregation."[36]

By focusing on our shared divine heritage as children of God, we can overcome prejudices and work toward unity. It's essential to approach others with empathy and understanding, especially when differences arise.

As President Nelson further counseled: "Building bridges of understanding will require much more of you, but that is exactly what your friend needs. Contention drives away the Spirit—every time."[37]

In our daily interactions, we have the opportunity to be peacemakers, to choose reconciliation over contention, and to build

---

36. Russell M. Nelson, *Building Bridges*, address given on June 1, 2018, at "Be One," the fortieth anniversary celebration of the 1978 revelation on the priesthood.

37. President Russell M. Nelson, *Peacemakers Needed*, General Conference (Salt Lake City: The Church of Jesus Christ of Latter-day Saints), April 2023, Gospel Library App.

communities rooted in love and mutual respect. By doing so, we not only strengthen our own faith but also inspire and uplift those around us.

When we create gospel-centered friendships, we become part of something greater: A community that reflects Christ's love and unites us in our shared purpose.

*Laís Gonçalves*

## Questions to Ponder

- How can I be more intentional in creating friendships that uplift, strengthen faith, and encourage mutual growth?
- Have I ever looked back on a difficult experience and realized that God had placed me exactly where I needed to be? How can I better trust His plan moving forward?
- What holds me back from sharing my testimony with others, and how can I overcome that fear or hesitation?

# Part IV

# Work and Purpose

# 13

# Finding Purpose Through Scripture

## Identifying your God-Given Mission and Calling

I HAVE SEEN MANY MIRACLES IN MY LIFE. I HAVE BEEN GUIDED BY THE Lord in ways I can't deny. Yet, for a long time, I wondered, "What is my true purpose?"

It may seem ironic that, despite seeing the Lord's hand so clearly, I never felt like I had a definitive answer to my life's mission. However, one experience changed my perspective.

I learned that our purpose is not always a single destination but a constant effort to align ourselves with the Lord's will. Purpose is not something we arrive at once and for all—but something we discover and rediscover as we seek to walk the Savior's path.

### A New Chapter in the United States

In 2014, I moved to the United States after getting married. My husband was preparing to continue his studies in Utah, and we had made the decision to build our future together here.

At first, the plan was clear. We would finish our studies and prepare to return to Brazil. But as time passed, things changed.

I had just returned from serving a full-time mission, a time in my life when I felt I was exactly where I needed to be every single day.

I had so many déjà vu moments on my mission—instances where I felt like I had already seen and felt those moments before. I had no doubt that I was where and when I was meant to be.

So, moving to another country so soon after my mission was a big shift. In less than a year, my life had completely changed—from missionary service to marriage, then from marriage to moving abroad and adapting to a new culture.

It was ironic because when I submitted my mission papers, I specifically checked the box saying I didn't want to learn a new language. I even left a note asking to serve among my own people.

Yet, here I was, in another country, speaking a different language.

## Discovering Purpose in Unexpected Places

As I adjusted to life in the U.S., I was called to serve in the Young Women organization. It was a wonderful experience where I learned more about the culture, the teenagers, their interests, their music, their lifestyle—everything.

But deep inside, I had this lingering feeling, this anxiety. I wanted to go back to serve my own people in Brazil.

Then, something happened that completely changed my understanding of purpose.

I was called to teach the Gospel Principles class—a class that focused on new members and those investigating the gospel.

At the time, I didn't know that this was the last year this specific class would be included in the Church curriculum. Looking back, I feel incredibly grateful that I was able to teach it before it was discontinued.

That year was transformative for me.

I met people from all walks of life—individuals who had been led by the Lord to that very place, in that very time.

Each person had a unique story, a path that led them to the gospel, and I got to hear their testimonies, struggles, and miracles.

## The Lord Knows Our Righteous Desires

I had always longed to serve my native people—the ones I had grown up with, those who spoke my language, those who shared my culture.

What I didn't realize at the time was that the Lord had granted me that desire—just in a different way.

Many of the people in my Gospel Principles class were from my home country. Some were from other countries but spoke my language.

The Lord had placed me exactly where I needed to be—not based on what I had imagined, but based on His greater plan.

I learned that purpose is not about geography. It's about the people God places in our path.

It was humbling to see their first encounters with the gospel, to watch them hear eternal truths for the first time, and to be a small part of their spiritual journey.

## The Book of Mormon and Our Purpose

Through that experience, I found a profound truth about purpose—sharing the gospel and testifying of Jesus Christ is one of the greatest callings we have in this life.

Whether it's with friends, family, acquaintances, newly baptized members, or our own children, we are all called to share what we know.

This is what brings true joy—being part of someone's journey back to the Savior.

The Book of Mormon has taught me this purpose time and time again. The book's very introduction states: "The Book of Mormon was written by way of commandment, and also by the spirit of prophecy and revelation . . . to the convincing of Jew and Gentile that Jesus is the Christ, the Eternal God."

The Book of Mormon exists so that all men and women may come unto Christ.

If that is its purpose, then that is also our purpose—to help others return to Him.

## A Challenge for You

If you are still searching for your purpose, I invite you to do the following:

- **Pray every day for guidance.** Ask God to help you recognize your purpose in the small things.
- **Study your patriarchal blessing.** Look for ways you can act on the promises and counsel found in it.
- **Write down impressions.** Keep a spiritual journal where you record moments when you feel God guiding you.
- **Take action.** Look for opportunities to serve, even in simple ways. Purpose is found in doing.
- **Be patient.** Trust that your purpose is unfolding in God's perfect timing.

As you do this, you will begin to see God's hand in your life more clearly. You will recognize that you have always had a purpose—you just needed to see it through His eyes.

And just like Nephi, you will be able to say with confidence: "I will go and do the things which the Lord hath commanded."[38]

*Laís Gonçalves*

## Questions to Ponder

- In what ways has the Lord already placed you in situations where you can fulfill a purpose, even if it wasn't what you initially expected?
- How can you better align your daily actions with the Lord's will so that He can reveal more of your purpose to you?

38. 1 Nephi 3:7.

# 14
# Scriptural Insights for Work Ethics

WORK IS A HUGE PART OF OUR MORTAL JOURNEY—AND NOT JUST IN the "I have to pay my bills" way, but in a much deeper, spiritual way. Our Heavenly Father designed work to be an essential part of our growth and progression. The scriptures are packed with wisdom on how to work with integrity, diligence, and excellence. As disciples of Jesus Christ, we're reminded to work "heartily, as to the Lord, and not unto men."[39] That means no slacking, no cutting corners—just giving our best effort, not because a boss is watching, but because *He* is.

Work is not merely a temporal necessity but a spiritual duty. From the Creation of the world, God established work as a fundamental part of human existence, as seen in Genesis 2:15: "And the Lord God took the man, and put him into the Garden of Eden to dress it and to keep it." This divine expectation continues today, requiring us to be honest in our dealings, diligent in our efforts, and excellent in our service.

39. Colossians 3:23.

## Integrity

The principle of integrity is foundational to our covenant relationship with God. In Doctrine and Covenants 97:8, the Lord declares:

> Verily I say unto you, all among them who know their hearts are honest, and are broken, and their spirits contrite, and are willing to observe their covenants by sacrifice—yea, every sacrifice which I, the Lord, shall command—they are accepted of me.

Integrity in the workplace means being truthful in our dealings, keeping our commitments, and standing firm in righteousness even when faced with temptation. Honesty also brings peace of mind. President James E. Faust taught, "Honesty is more than not lying. It is truth-telling, truth-speaking, truth-living, and truth-loving."[40] When we live with integrity and honesty, we invite the Spirit into our lives and build a reputation of trustworthiness that blesses not only ourselves but those around us.

Elder Kim B. Clark, in his address *Becoming a Disciple-Leader*, emphasized that leadership is inherently a moral work, seeking to do good and make things better for people in the long term. He stated, "Leaders always seek to make things better and to do good. This is the soul of leadership."[41] This perspective aligns closely with the principle of integrity, as it underscores the moral responsibility we have in our interactions and decisions as disciples of Jesus Christ.

Now, I work in a university department that handles Academic Honesty cases. I've seen students get caught cheating, and I'll be honest—when I first started, I thought about dishonesty in black and white terms. If someone cheated, they should deal with the consequences. But as I started working more closely with the students, I realized that many of them weren't trying to be dishonest for the sake of being dishonest. Some were overwhelmed with depression and anxiety. Others had just lost a loved one. Some had been through awful

40. James E Faust, *Honesty—a Moral Compass*, General Conference (Salt Lake City: The Church of Jesus Christ of Latter-day Saints), October 1996, Gospel Library App.

41. Kim B. Clark, *Becoming a Disciple-Leader*, BYU Devotional, July 30th, 2024, https://speeches.byu.edu/talks/kim-b-clark/becoming-a-disciple-leader/.

situations like domestic violence or a divorce. And in their desperation, they made a bad choice.

That changed how I saw integrity—not as a rigid rule to punish people, but as an opportunity to teach, lift, and help people find *a better way*. Of course, some students cheat because they think they can get away with it, but for a lot of them, dishonesty comes from fear, stress, and not knowing what else to do. And that's exactly how Satan works. He convinces us that we're stuck, that lying is our only way out. But that's never true. There is always another way.

To cultivate integrity, we must:

- Speak the truth in all circumstances (Doctrine and Covenants 42:21)
- Refuse to participate in deceitful practices (Proverbs 11:1)
- Keep our commitments and honor our word (Matthew 5:37)

## Diligence

Diligence is a divine trait that reflects our faithfulness in fulfilling our responsibilities. Doctrine and Covenants 107:99 instructs, "Wherefore, now let every man learn his duty, and to act in the office in which he is appointed, in all diligence."

The Lord requires effort from His disciples. He does not expect perfection, but He does expect persistence. Elder David A. Bednar taught, "Ordinary people who faithfully, diligently, and consistently do simple things that are right before God will bring forth extraordinary results."[42] Small, daily efforts lead to long-term success.

Nephi is a great example of diligence. When he declared, "I will go and do the things which the Lord hath commanded" (1 Nephi 3:7), he meant it—and he followed through, even when things got hard. He didn't quit. He kept trying. Likewise, we're expected to work with purpose, patience, and perseverance.

But diligence isn't just about how we show up for ourselves. It's also about how we show up for others. Discipleship is not a solo gig.

42. David A. Bednar, *'By Small and Simple Things Are Great Things Brought to Pass' (Alma 37:6–7)*, Brigham Young University Women's Conference address, April 29, 2011, 2, ce.byu.edu/cw/womensconference/pdf/archive/2011/Elder_David_A._Bednar.pdf.

Elder Kim B. Clark introduced a concept called "power through" discipleship. Unlike "power over" approaches that rely on control or authority, "power through" means lifting and strengthening others by activating the power within them. That kind of discipleship takes consistent effort. It means we engage, encourage, and empower people as they grow in their own relationship with Christ.

Elder Clark's message expands our view of what it means to be a diligent disciple. It's not just about grinding through our to-do list. It's about ministering with purpose—patiently, humbly, and consistently. It's about helping others access the divine power already inside them. In doing so, we follow the Savior, who ministered one by one, lifting hearts and changing lives.

Now, let me be real for a second. Diligence is hard for me. I have a lot of the same challenges people with ADHD face—difficulty focusing, forgetting things, struggling with time management, and just generally getting distracted *all the time.* Growing up, this looked like laziness to a lot of people. I was told I wasn't trying hard enough when, in reality, my brain just isn't wired like everyone else's.

As an adult, I've learned ways to work *with* my brain instead of against it. There is a list of things that help me stay diligent:

- **Structured Routines**—I use planners, digital reminders, and set schedules to keep myself on track
- **Breaking Tasks into Smaller Steps**—Instead of getting overwhelmed by big projects, I focus on one tiny step at a time
- **Minimizing Distractions**—Noise-canceling headphones and focus apps are lifesavers
- **Timers**—The Pomodoro Technique (work for 25–30 minutes, then take a break) helps me stay on task
- **Accountability**—Checking in with a friend or mentor keeps me motivated

Diligence isn't about being flawless. It's about showing up, doing your best, and staying with it—even when it's messy, even when it's hard. As someone wise (and animated) once said: "Just keep swimming. Just keep swimming."

## Excellence

Excellence is the pursuit of our divine potential in all that we do. The Lord expects us to magnify our talents and develop our abilities for the benefit of His kingdom. In Matthew 25:14–30, the parable of the talents teaches the importance of diligence and wise stewardship over the gifts God has given us.

President Russell M. Nelson has emphasized the importance of seeking excellence in our work: "The Lord loves effort, because effort brings rewards that can't come without it."[43]

Striving for excellence extends beyond our professional work and includes our service in the Church. Whether we are called to be a leader, a teacher, a nursery worker, or the person who folds chairs after meetings, we should approach each calling with the same commitment and devotion. Every role in the Lord's kingdom has purpose and meaning. President Thomas S. Monson taught, "When we are on the Lord's errand, we are entitled to the Lord's help."[44]

While on the Lord's errand, we are not just called to lead. We are called to lead as true disciples of Jesus Christ. A disciple-leader, a term introduced by Kim B. Clark, is someone who follows the Savior's example in both heart and action, striving to serve others with humility, love, and dedication. This means that leadership in the Church is not about authority for its own sake; it is about ministering, lifting, and inspiring others to come unto Christ.

A disciple-leader does more than the bare minimum. They prepare lessons with care, arrive early to set up, make visitors feel welcome, pray for those they teach, and magnify even the smallest responsibility. They seek excellence in every aspect of their life, not for personal gain, but to bless and uplift those they serve. Excellence in

---

43. Joy D. Jones, *An Especially Noble Calling*, General Conference (Salt Lake City: The Church of Jesus Christ of Latter-day Saints), April 2020 (Jones presents a video recording of President Nelson speaking to children).

44. President Thomas S. Monson, *To Learn, to Do, to Be*, General Conference (Salt Lake City: The Church of Jesus Christ of Latter-day Saints), October 2008, Gospel Library App.

our Church callings is about doing everything "with an eye single to the glory of God."[45]

Striving for excellence also means seeking to improve ourselves intellectually, spiritually, and physically. The Lord expects us to grow and develop in ways that allow us to contribute more effectively to His work. Doctrine and Covenants 130:18 teaches: "Whatever principle of intelligence we attain unto in this life, it will rise with us in the resurrection."

A commitment to lifelong learning is part of achieving excellence. This could mean improving our skills, furthering our education, developing Christlike attributes, or even refining talents such as music, art, or writing to inspire others.

Regardless of our profession or occupation, excellence means treating our work as a sacred stewardship. Whether we are teachers, business professionals, parents, students, or service workers, we should work "heartily, as to the Lord."[46]

At the end of the day, our work—both in our careers and in the gospel—is an opportunity to grow. When we live with integrity, we build trust. When we work diligently, we make progress. When we strive for excellence, we magnify our talents.

God sees our efforts, even the small ones. He strengthens us when we struggle, guides us when we're lost, and helps us achieve more than we ever thought possible. So let's commit to working heartily, being honest, and giving our best—not just for a paycheck, but because it's part of who we are meant to be.

*Ana de Castro*

## Questions to Ponder

- In what ways do I demonstrate integrity in my daily work and responsibilities?
- How do I handle situations where honesty is challenged?
- What strategies can I use to improve my diligence, especially when faced with distractions or discouragement?

---

45. Doctrine and Covenants 4:5.

46. Colossians 3:23.

- How can I magnify my talents and spiritual gifts to better serve in my work and Church callings?
- What are some small changes I can make to increase my personal and professional excellence?
- How does my work ethic reflect my commitment to discipleship? Am I a disciple-leader?
- What role does the Lord play in helping me develop integrity, diligence, and excellence?

# 15

# Balancing Work and Rest

## Understanding the Sabbath and Principles of Restorative Rest

THE STORY OF MARY AND MARTHA HAS ALWAYS RESONATED DEEPLY with me. In Luke 10:41–42, we read:

> And Jesus answered and said unto her, Martha, Martha, thou art careful and troubled about many things: But one thing is needful: and Mary hath chosen that good part, which shall not be taken away from her.

Martha, busy with preparations and overwhelmed by her responsibilities, represents the struggle so many of us face in our daily lives. We often fill our schedules with tasks, believing that productivity equates to worthiness. Yet, Jesus gently reminds Martha—and all of us—that while our responsibilities are important, they should not overshadow the need to be present and to nourish our souls. Martha's concern for the external—the physical—is valid, yet the Lord points out that her true need was internal—spiritual nourishment. The heart of this passage is a reminder that there is a higher calling than the demands of daily life.

Mary, sitting at the Savior's feet, embodies the essence of choosing the "good part." Her focus on spiritual connection and rest serves as a reminder of the importance of pausing amid the demands of life. In a world that glorifies busyness, this story calls us to reevaluate our priorities. Are we so consumed by our to-do lists that we miss the chance to meaningfully connect with God, our loved ones, and even ourselves?

## Learning to Pause

There was a season in my life when I worked a full-time job far from my hometown while attending college at night. Each day began with a 90-minute commute, and every hour was tightly scheduled as I tried to make ends meet and carry the weight of family responsibilities and callings. I filled my days from dawn until long past dark, taking pride in how much I could juggle. It was a badge of honor to be busy. After all, wasn't busyness a sign of success? But there came a point when the exhaustion caught up with me. My productivity felt hollow because I wasn't truly present for my family or myself. I was caught up in a cycle of doing, but I was neglecting the deeper, more meaningful aspects of life.

I remember one particularly grueling week when I barely saw my kids and felt disconnected from my husband. On Sunday, I collapsed on the couch, too tired to attend church, but I did it. That day, I realized something needed to change. I had been so busy "doing" that I had forgotten how to simply "be." The realization was sobering. My constant movement and endless task list had begun to steal the joy from my relationships and my spirit. I had become like Martha—so consumed by my responsibilities that I was losing sight of the purpose behind them.

This experience reminds me of Ramit Sethi's analogy about money: He often discusses how some individuals focus so heavily on saving that they neglect learning to spend money consciously and effectively. He advocates for identifying "Money Dials"—areas where you can splurge on things you love while cutting back on expenses that don't bring you joy, as outlined in *I Will Teach You to Be Rich*. This approach, called Conscious Spending, emphasizes allocating money according to your passions and values, rather than saving without a clear purpose. The same principle applies to work and rest. Working hard is valuable, but if we don't know how to pause and rest intentionally, we risk working endlessly without truly enjoying the fruits of our labor. We become so focused on the outcome—achieving the next goal, ticking off the next task—that we forget to appreciate the present moment. We miss the blessings of relationships, peace, and spiritual growth.

## The Sabbath: A Divine Gift of Rest

One of the most powerful tools God has given us to find balance is the Sabbath. In Exodus 20:8, the Lord commands: "Remember the sabbath day, to keep it holy."

The Sabbath is not just a day of rest but a day of restoration, a time to realign our priorities and reconnect with God. President Russell M. Nelson described the Sabbath as a "delight," emphasizing the spiritual renewal it offers: "Faith in God engenders a love for the Sabbath; faith in the Sabbath engenders a love for God. A sacred Sabbath truly is a delight."[47]

When we honor the Sabbath by setting aside our labors, we allow ourselves to recharge spiritually, mentally, and physically. It is a chance to step away from the world's demands and focus on what truly matters—our relationship with God, our loved ones, and ourselves. The Sabbath is a sacred pause that enables us to find balance in our lives. By resting and refraining from work, we create space for the things that matter most—nourishing our souls, strengthening our families, and deepening our connection with our Heavenly Father.

The Sabbath offers us an invitation to stop and take a step back from the world's distractions. It is an invitation to look inward and upward, to remember the blessings we have received, and to reflect on our relationship with God. For many of us, this time of rest may be the only period in the week when we are able to quiet the noise of the world and focus on our spiritual well-being.

---

47. Russell M. Nelson, *The Sabbath Is a Delight*, General Conference (Salt Lake City: The Church of Jesus Christ of Latter-day Saints), April 2015, Gospel Library App.

## The Science of Rest

Modern research confirms what the Lord has taught us about the importance of rest. Studies show that regular periods of rest and reflection improve productivity, creativity, and overall well-being. Neuroscience reveals that our brains function best when we alternate between focused work and deliberate rest. Rest is not only restorative; it enhances our cognitive function, boosts creativity, and increases our overall efficiency. It is an essential component of a healthy, balanced life.

In his book *Rest: Why You Get More Done When You Work Less*, Alex Soojung-Kim Pang explains that rest is not a luxury but a necessity. He writes, "Deliberate rest helps us recover from stress, allows us to process and solidify what we've learned, and gives us the opportunity to think more creatively."[48] In essence, rest helps us become better versions of ourselves—more focused, more creative, and more capable of handling life's demands.

Similarly, just as our bodies require physical rest, our spirits need spiritual rest. Elder Jeffrey R. Holland spoke of this need, saying: "Fatigue is the common enemy of us all—so slow down, rest up, replenish, and refill."[49]

When we are spiritually fatigued, we risk losing our ability to connect with God and others. Spiritual rest, through practices such as prayer, meditation, scripture study, and worship, allows us to recharge our inner selves. These moments of stillness help us regain our spiritual strength and prepare us to face the challenges of life with renewed energy and perspective.

## Balancing Work and Rest

Finding the balance between work and rest requires intentionality. The world often celebrates busyness, but the gospel teaches us that true success lies in balance. Thomas S. Monson once said, quoting

---

48. Alex Soojung-Kim Pang, *Rest: Why You Get More Done When You Work Less* [New York: Basic Books, 2016], 11.

49. Jeffrey R. Holland, *Like a Broken Vessel,* General Conference (Salt Lake City: The Church of Jesus Christ of Latter-day Saints), October 2013, Gospel Library App.

President Gordon B. Hinckley: "Strive to serve. Vision without work is daydreaming. Work without vision is drudgery. But work coupled with vision shall yield to you the success you desire."[50]

The key is not to avoid work—it is to approach work with purpose and integrate periods of rest to maintain our physical, emotional, and spiritual health. Rest is not a sign of weakness; it is an acknowledgment of our divine design. Just as we are designed to work, we are also designed to rest. The balance between work and rest is where we find harmony.

In my own life, I've learned that setting aside time for rest is not a luxury but a necessity. By intentionally scheduling time for rest—whether through prayer, relaxation, or spending time with loved ones—I create space for the things that matter most. As Elder Dieter F. Uchtdorf taught, "We need not be anxious about what we cannot control; rather, we should focus our energy on the things that matter most."[51] I've found that taking time to rest not only makes me more productive in the long run but also enriches my relationships and strengthens my faith.

## Practical Steps for Restorative Rest

Here are some ways to incorporate balance and rest into your life:

- **Honor the Sabbath:** Dedicate the Sabbath to worship, rest, and connection with family. Avoid unnecessary labor and focus on activities that bring spiritual renewal. The Sabbath is a sacred gift that provides us with a weekly opportunity to realign our priorities and rest in the presence of God.
- **Schedule Rest:** Just as you schedule work, schedule time for rest. This can include daily breaks, weekly pauses, or even vacations. Deliberate rest helps you recharge and perform

---

50. Church News Archives, *Church News: A Living Record of the Restoration*, Archives, "'Vision without work is daydreaming,'" May 13, 2000. https://www.thechurchnews.com/2000/5/13/23246515/vision-without-work-is-daydreaming/.

51. Dieter F. Uchtdorf, *Of Things That Matter Most*, General Conference (Salt Lake City: The Church of Jesus Christ of Latter-day Saints), October 2010, Gospel Library App.

better. Make rest a priority in your life, and don't feel guilty for taking the time you need to replenish.

- **Embrace Presence Over Productivity:** Learn to set aside distractions and focus on the moment. Whether it's dinner with your family or personal scripture study, being fully present brings peace and fulfillment. The quality of our relationships is far more important than the quantity of tasks we can complete in a day.
- **Practice Gratitude:** Rest isn't just physical. It's emotional and spiritual. Reflect on your blessings daily to cultivate a sense of peace and balance. Gratitude helps shift our focus from what we don't have to what we've been given, fostering contentment and joy.
- **Incorporate Calm Music and Meditation:** Listening to calm, uplifting music or practicing meditation can quiet the mind and create space for spiritual impressions. These moments of stillness help us focus on receiving revelation and aligning our lives with God's will. As Loren G. Dalton reminds us, "You are receiving revelation; now act on it" (Dalton, 2019).
- **Set Boundaries:** Just as you protect your time for work, protect your time for rest. Learn to say no to excessive commitments and prioritize wisely. Setting clear boundaries is essential to protecting our time and energy, enabling us to focus on what truly matters (Cloud & Townsend, 1992).
- **Reevaluate Priorities Regularly:** Take time to assess your schedule and ensure it aligns with your values. If work is overshadowing your relationships or spiritual growth, it may be time to make adjustments. Reevaluate your priorities and make intentional changes to create more balance in your life.

## Choosing the "Good Part"

The story of Mary and Martha reminds us that balance is about more than just managing time: It's about tending what you want to grow. Just like a farmer plants seeds, waters the soil, and patiently cares for the crop every day. When we consistently nurture our priorities, we see them flourish. As we strive to balance work and rest, we can take inspiration from Mary, who chose to sit at the Savior's feet and be nourished spiritually. Mary understood that in order to truly serve, she first needed to rest and connect with the Savior.

When we honor the Sabbath, prioritize rest, and embrace presence over productivity, we are choosing the "good part." We are reminding ourselves that our worth is not measured by how much we accomplish, but by our connection to God and to those we love. As President Nelson taught, "We need to do better and be better because we are in a battle." [52]

Let us follow His example by balancing our efforts with meaningful rest, creating lives that are both productive and deeply fulfilling.

*Caroline Melazzo*

## Questions to Ponder

- Am I living like Martha, caught up in the demands of daily life and neglecting my spiritual well-being? How can I make room for more intentional rest and connection with God?
- What would it look like for me to "choose the good part" in my own life? How can I prioritize spiritual nourishment over busyness?
- How can I better honor the Sabbath in my own life? What steps can I take to make it a day of spiritual restoration?
- How am I balancing work and rest? Am I giving myself permission to rest without guilt?
- What boundaries do I need to set in my life to create more balance between work and rest?
- In what areas of my life do I need to focus on presence over productivity? How can I be more present in my relationships with God and others?

52. Russell M. Nelson, *We Can Do Better and Be Better,* General Conference (Salt Lake City: The Church of Jesus Christ of Latter-day Saints), April 2019, Gospel Library App.

# 16

# Generosity and Stewardship

## Managing Resources According to Scriptural Teachings

When my husband Bruno and I first arrived in Idaho, our financial situation felt . . . uncertain. We had carefully planned our move, but no amount of preparation can erase the unknowns that come with starting over in a new place.

Bruno was about to begin his first semester at BYU–Idaho, and we knew tuition alone would take a big chunk of our savings. On top of that, we had rent, groceries, and all the little costs that come with adjusting to a new environment.

We weren't in a desperate situation—we had been careful with our resources—but there was still this constant awareness that we couldn't afford to make mistakes. Every dollar mattered, and every financial decision felt weighty.

Yet, one decision had already been made—one we wouldn't compromise on: to always pay our tithing and be generous in our fast offerings.

Paying tithing had always been a priority for us. It wasn't something we debated, even when money was tight. We believed the Lord's promise in Malachi:

> Bring ye all the tithes into the storehouse . . . and prove me now herewith . . . if I will not open you the windows of heaven, and pour you out a blessing, that there shall not be room enough to receive it.[53]

But this time, being generous in our offerings felt like an especially bold act of faith. Parting with that money, knowing we had other expenses ahead, made me pause. Yet we knew what we had to do.

I remember writing the check for our tithing and offerings, followed by the payment for tuition. There was no immediate miracle—no sudden relief—but I felt peace. I knew we had done what the Lord had asked, and that was enough.

What I didn't know was that God was already preparing to bless us in ways we never expected.

## The Lord Had a Plan All Along

Both Bruno and I were working hard. I was still employed in Brazil, working from home—which meant waking up at 4 a.m. to align with their office hours. Bruno was just as dedicated, staying up until 11 p.m. most nights, studying endlessly to maintain his grades. His goal was to earn a merit-based scholarship for the following semester by maintaining a 4.0 GPA, but that was still months away.

A few months earlier, before moving to the U.S., we had visited my former bishop from before we were married. He gave us one simple yet profound piece of counsel: "Never stop paying your tithes. Trust the Lord, and be generous in your fast offerings."

That advice stayed with us—and we held onto it, even when finances felt uncertain.

About a month after we arrived in Idaho, Bruno took a chance and applied for financial aid. We didn't expect much, but we knew we had to try.

53. Malachi 3:10.

Then came the surprise—a blessing we hadn't even known to pray for.

We learned that Bruno had been awarded an international scholarship, one we hadn't realized existed! The amount was substantial—half of what we had already paid to cover the first two semesters' tuition. We were stunned.

The Lord had provided.

The refund allowed us to buy a four-wheel-drive vehicle for the snowy Rexburg roads—a car that was in great condition for its low value, and that remains with us still today.

The following semester, Bruno's relentless dedication to his studies paid off. This time, he qualified for a merit-based scholarship. This followed until the end of his studies, receiving a full scholarship for every semester.

Those moments—receiving two unexpected scholarships—felt like the Lord reminding us, "I see you. I know your sacrifices. And I will provide."

## Living by Faith and Generosity

Our commitment to tithing was never a question of *if.* It was always a question of *how much more generous can we be?*

The Lord didn't just bless us financially; He opened countless other doors—including professional ones.

- Bruno was hired at the university, in his field of expertise, less than a month into his first semester.
- Eight months later, he was invited to interview for an internship he hadn't even applied for.
- We were also approved to live in subsidized housing, lowering our expenses significantly.
- After graduating—and having worked full-time for the same company he interned for—Bruno received a job offer in Utah, close to the family and friends we had long hoped to live near.

Looking back, we can see how each opportunity—each unexpected blessing—was directly tied to our faith and the trust we had placed in the Lord's promises.

One of the greatest blessings has been seeing how the Lord's timing—even when it didn't match our own—was always perfect. Our visa process unfolded at just the right time, our resources always seemed to be enough, and Bruno's career has continued to progress in remarkable ways.

## Lessons from the Tuition Miracle

I've learned that the Lord's blessings often come in ways we don't expect, and regularly come *after* we've shown our willingness to trust Him.

I realized that paying tithing isn't about what we give. It's about what we receive:

- **Peace** that comes from knowing we've done our part
- **Confidence** that God will provide
- **Faith** that His timing is better than ours

Just like the Savior's parable of the talents, where the faithful servants were rewarded for wisely multiplying what they had been given,[54] I've seen God multiply our efforts when we acted with faith.

Being wise stewards of our resources—by planning carefully, trusting God, and being willing to give—has shaped our family's journey in ways we could never have imagined.

I know that when we put the Lord first, He truly does "open the windows of heaven."[55] Not always in the way we expect—but always in the way we need most.

*Letícia Araujo*

## Questions to Ponder

If you're facing financial uncertainty, I invite you to test the Lord's promise. Begin by asking yourself:

- Am I trusting the Lord with my resources?
- Am I seeking to be generous with what I have—whether large or small?

54. Matthew 25:14–30.

55. Malachi 3:10.

- Do I recognize and express gratitude for the blessings I've already received?

As you strive to trust Him, I know He will bless you in ways you may not expect, but in ways that will strengthen your faith and bring you peace.

"For ye receive no witness until after the trial of your faith."[56]

56. Ether 12:6.

# Part V

# Navigating Life's Challenges

# 17

# Overcoming Temptation

## Strategies for Resisting Negative Influences Through Scripture

### Resisting Negative Influences Online

THE DIGITAL WORLD OFFERS INCREDIBLE OPPORTUNITIES FOR CONnection, learning, and inspiration, but it also presents unique challenges. The constant exposure to curated perfection, peer pressure, and temptations through social media and entertainment make standing firm in our beliefs more difficult than ever. How can we navigate these challenges while staying true to our faith?

### Learning from Personal Experience

Beyond the thrill of performing, dance taught me discipline and responsibility. I treated my training as seriously as I did my goals in the Church's Personal Progress program. But as much as I loved dancing, my journey wasn't without challenges. I faced moments when I had to choose between my passion for dance and my commitment to my beliefs. Sundays, for example, were often filled with rehearsals or performances, and I felt torn between my desire to dance and my need to honor Heavenly Father. I often talked to my ballet teacher and fellow dancers about these struggles, and their support surprised me. Over time, some of my dance friends even joined the Church and later expressed how much they respected my choices, reminding me how our examples touch others in ways we might not realize.

Friendship was incredibly important to me during this time. I was lucky to have friends from church who shared my values. Together, we studied the scriptures and encouraged each other spiritually. Our bonds were rooted in respect, modesty, and shared beliefs, which made navigating the ups and downs of adolescence easier. But I also had other friends from dance and school who didn't share my beliefs, and sometimes that brought its own challenges.

As teenagers, we all had our crushes, went on trips together, and loved to have fun. But I often found myself standing out when it came to my choices of clothes or music. Many of my friends wanted to wear revealing outfits that I didn't feel comfortable in, especially on trips or at parties. I remember how difficult it was to balance wanting to fit in with staying true to my values. I loved fashion—always have. But for me, fashion and modesty had to go hand in hand. I wasn't just dressing for myself; I was representing my beliefs and honoring my Heavenly Father. My friends didn't always understand why I wouldn't wear certain clothes, but over time, I found ways to express my personal style in a way that was both fashionable and modest. I realized that modesty wasn't about denying my femininity, but rather about enhancing it with grace and respect.

Music was another area where I felt this tension. I loved dancing, and sometimes the rhythms and beats of a song were so good it was hard to resist moving to the music. But when the lyrics were "depraved," as we say in Portuguese, I couldn't bring myself to dance to it. It didn't feel right. I've always believed that the Spirit can't dwell in a space where disrespectful or vulgar influences take over. In those moments, I had to make hard choices. I chose to walk away from certain songs, clothes, and situations—even when my friends didn't understand.

The lessons I learned through dance have stayed with me throughout my life. Dance is not only a physical art; it requires emotional and spiritual engagement. It taught me how to express myself through movement, but it also taught me the importance of maintaining my values in the face of temptation. Whether it was choosing modesty over trends or refusing to dance to music with inappropriate lyrics, I learned that being true to myself was more important than fitting in. This was a valuable lesson that extended beyond the dance studio and into every aspect of my life—especially in a world that often pressures us to conform.

## The Psychology of Standing Alone

Resisting temptation and standing alone in our values is not just a spiritual challenge, b a psychological one. Research in psychology highlights the difficulty of resisting peer influence, especially in adolescence. Studies show that peer pressure activates the brain's reward center, making conformity feel rewarding, while standing alone can feel isolating and stressful. However, research also shows that those who practice moral courage—standing firm in their beliefs despite opposition—develop greater resilience and emotional strength over time.

A study published in the *Journal of Adolescence* by Steinberg and Monahan (2007)[57] explored how teenagers develop resistance to negative peer influence as they grow older. Their research found that adolescents who consistently resist such pressure tend to have higher self-esteem, greater emotional intelligence, and a clearer sense of personal identity. While standing alone against peer pressure can be difficult in the moment, this resilience fosters long-term psychological strength and confidence. Developing the ability to say no to harmful influences ultimately helps young people grow into more secure and self-aware adults.

Moreover, research in psychology[58] indicates that making values-based decisions—choices aligned with personal priorities and core beliefs—is strongly linked to lower levels of stress and regret[1]. When we make choices that reflect our true values, we feel grounded and confident, reducing second-guessing and anxiety about our decisions.

---

57. Laurence Steinberg and Kathryn C Monahan, "Age Differences in Resistance to peer Influence," *Developmental Psychology*, 43(6), 2007, 1531-1543, https://doi.org/10.1037/0012-1649.43.6.1531.

58. Claude M. Steele, "The Psychology of Self-affirmation: Sustaining the Integrity of the Self, *Advances in Experimental Social Psychology*, 21, 1988, 261–302, https://doi.org/10.1016/S0065-2601(08)60229-4.

When we choose to live according to our faith, even in a virtual world filled with temptations, we reinforce our self-worth and align our actions with our core values, leading to greater personal fulfillment and spiritual peace.

Standing firm in our values may feel difficult or isolating at times, but it also empowers us to become stronger and more resilient. As we continue to practice moral courage, we develop a deeper sense of self-worth and a clearer understanding of who we are. This inner strength enables us to confidently face challenges, whether they come from friends, family, or the digital world.

## Finding Courage in the Virtual World

Today, those same challenges exist but in a different form. Instead of just peer pressure at school or among friends, young people face an online world full of temptations and difficult choices. Social media, for example, can be both a source of good and a space where we are constantly bombarded with unrealistic standards, negative influences, and unwholesome content.

It takes courage to stand alone online—to unfollow accounts that don't align with our values, to resist the pressure to engage in gossip or negativity, and to choose uplifting media. The same principles that guided me in my dance journey apply to how we navigate the digital world today: being mindful of what we consume, who we interact with, and how we represent ourselves.

When I was growing up, our interactions were limited to face-to-face conversations and phone calls. Today, however, young people are constantly connected through social media platforms. These platforms, while offering amazing opportunities to connect with others, can also be a breeding ground for comparison, insecurity, and unhealthy pressures. The curated nature of social media often leads to a distorted view of reality. It's easy to believe that everyone else is living a perfect, carefree life while we struggle with our own challenges. In a world that constantly tells us we aren't enough, it's essential to develop the strength to stand firm in our identity and values.

Social media often amplifies negative influences. Whether it's to beauty standards, opinions, or lifestyles, the pressure to conform is heightened in the digital world. But this is where we can find courage—by taking control of our online experience. It takes strength to set boundaries, unfollow accounts that spread negativity, and resist the temptation to compare ourselves to others. By curating our digital environment and choosing to engage with content that uplifts and inspires, we can create a space that aligns with our values and supports our spiritual growth.

## A Scriptural Example of Standing Alone

One of the most powerful scriptural examples of resisting temptation and standing alone is Daniel. Taken from his homeland and immersed in the foreign culture of Babylon, Daniel is surrounded by people who do not share his beliefs. He is offered the king's meat and wine, which goes against the dietary laws of his faith. Despite being in a position where it would have been easier to conform, Daniel courageously refuses and requests a diet aligned with his values. His commitment is later blessed as he and his friends appear healthier and stronger than those who had indulged in the king's food.[59]

Daniel's story mirrors the challenges we face in the virtual world. There are moments when we must decide whether to consume the content that the world is offering or stand firm in what we know is right. Sometimes, that means unfollowing influencers who promote lifestyles contrary to our beliefs. Other times, it means standing alone when others are engaging in inappropriate discussions or trends online. Like Daniel, we are called to be different, and though it may feel isolating, the Lord blesses those who choose righteousness.

Just as Daniel stood firm in his commitment to his faith despite the pressures of Babylon, we can stand firm in our values despite the pressures of the digital world. We may feel like we are standing alone at times, but God promises to bless those who choose to remain faithful. Like Daniel, we can experience spiritual strength and blessings when we make choices that align with our faith, even in the face of opposition.

## Strategies for Overcoming Digital Temptations

To successfully navigate the digital world while standing firm in our beliefs, we need to employ specific strategies:

59. Daniel 1:8–16.

- **Curate Your Social Media Feed**—Be intentional about who you follow. Seek out content that uplifts, educates, and inspires rather than content that fosters negativity or temptation.
- **Set Screen Time Limits**—Spending too much time on social media can expose us to more temptations and distractions. Setting time limits can help maintain a healthy balance.
- **Surround Yourself with Virtuous Content**—Listen to uplifting music, watch wholesome shows, and engage in positive discussions that strengthen rather than diminish your faith.
- **Be Mindful of Your Online Interactions**—Avoid engaging in gossip, arguments, or content that does not reflect the standards of a disciple of Christ.
- **Pray for Strength and Discernment**—Just as Daniel relied on God, we can turn to Him for guidance and strength in navigating the challenges of the digital world.

## The Courage to Stand Alone

It is not always easy to be different, especially in a world that constantly encourages conformity. But just as I learned in my dance journey, staying true to our beliefs not only strengthens us but can also be an example to others. Social media may be a part of our daily lives, but we can choose to use it in ways that align with our faith.

As President Thomas S. Monson once said, "Dare to stand alone. Dare to have a purpose firm; Dare to make it known."[60]

By making wise choices in the digital world, we uphold our values, protect our spiritual well-being, and ultimately grow closer to God. The courage to stand alone isn't just about rejecting the bad. It's about embracing the good and choosing to be a light in an ever-darkening world.

*Caroline Melazzo*

---

60. President Tomas S. Monson, *Dare to Stand Alone,* General Conference (Salt Lake City: The Church of Jesus Christ of Latter-day Saints), October 2011, Gospel Library App.

## Questions to Ponder

- In what ways has peer pressure, either online or offline, affected my decisions? How can I stand firm in my values in these situations?
- How can I better curate my digital environment to align with my beliefs and values?
- What are some strategies I can use to avoid negative influences on social media?
- How can I follow Daniel's example of standing firm in my faith, even when others around me may not share my beliefs?
- What does it mean to stand alone in the digital world, and how can I find strength in doing so?
- How can I support my friends and family in their efforts to stand firm in their beliefs, both online and offline?

# 18

# Faith in Times of Suffering

## Finding Hope and Perseverance in Challenging Circumstances

### A Season of Uncertainty

The early years of our marriage were filled with love but also with challenges that tested our faith. My husband made the decision to join the army, and while we waited for his basic training date, we faced an unexpected hurdle—his immigration status had to be changed. Because of this, he was unable to work for a period of time.

We had savings, and I was working as a personal assistant while caring for our first child, but financially, things became tight. Even though he couldn't earn an income, my husband continued to serve—volunteering at the Church office, wanting to keep his position and responsibilities until everything was resolved. It was humbling to watch him dedicate himself to service, trusting that things would eventually return to normal.

We had two cars at the time. One was an older model and fully paid off, which my husband used. The other was a newer car that I used while running errands with our son. We were doing our best to balance everything, trusting that the Lord was aware of our situation and would provide for us.

## The Forgotten Keys and the Weight of Fear

Through all of this we lived in an apartment complex with many different neighbors, and though I was familiar with some of them, I didn't know everyone well. Our next-door neighbors were new, and though I didn't know them personally, we had noticed some tension in their home—such as arguments and drinking. One day, in the middle of all this, I made a mistake that sent me into a spiral of worry.

I tend to be a bit forgetful, not because I don't pay attention, but because my mind is always processing so much at once. I hear everything, I notice everything, but focusing on just one thing can be difficult when my brain is constantly overstimulated. That day, I had been running errands, taking care of my son, and thinking about everything on my to-do list when I accidentally left my keys in the door of our apartment.

Hours passed before I even realized what had happened. By the time I did, the keys were gone.

Panic hit me.

I immediately feared the worst. Had someone taken my keys? What if they planned to steal my car? What if they could now get into our apartment?

I searched everywhere, retraced my steps, and asked around, but the keys were nowhere to be found. The anxiety of our financial situation, my responsibilities as a mother, and now this—this simple yet potentially disastrous mistake—felt overwhelming.

The day went by, and I still had no answers. No one had come to return the keys, no one had reached out, and I didn't want to worry my family about it.

## A Divine Assurance

Early the next morning, I stepped outside to the stairs of our apartment building, needing a moment to clear my mind. But instead of finding peace, I felt an unbearable loneliness. The weight of my worries crushed me, and I began to cry—hard.

I prayed desperately, pouring out my heart to the Lord.

Then, in that still, quiet moment, I heard it.

A voice.

It wasn't loud, yet it wasn't just a thought. It was spoken into my ears but pierced straight into my heart: "You are not alone."

It was as if the words filled my entire being. Suddenly, my fears didn't feel so heavy anymore.

At that moment, I felt an overwhelming strength take over. Instead of fear, I felt empowered. Instead of waiting, I knew I needed to act.

## Taking Action with Faith

With this newfound strength, I started knocking on my neighbors' doors.

One by one, I asked if anyone had seen my keys. Most people hadn't, but I wasn't discouraged. I knocked on another door, then another.

Finally, at one apartment, a soft-spoken teenage girl—likely not yet eighteen—opened the door slightly ajar. She asked how she could help. I explained my situation, and she hesitated for a moment before saying, "I did see some keys that might not be ours."

When she brought them out, I could hear the familiar jingle of my keychain before I even saw them. That sound—so specific and unmistakable—made my heart leap. I knew instantly and certainly: They were mine.

She handed them to me, and in that moment, I felt an indescribable relief. It was early in the morning, and I knew from experience that this particular home was usually full of life—but only much later in the day. I had often heard loud music, late-night arguments, and signs that the adults there kept a different schedule than mine. Because of that, I honestly didn't expect anyone to answer so early. But she did.

It's possible that someone else in her home had picked them up—maybe even with uncertain intentions. But that morning, she chose to respond. Her simple action—listening, checking, and helping—reminded me that the Lord often works through the quiet courage of others. Especially those we don't expect. She didn't need to understand the full story to be part of the answer to my prayer. And through her, I felt seen and remembered by a loving God.

This moment touched something deeper in me; it brushed up against my fears, my assumptions, and even my faith. I had started to drown in negative thoughts, drawing conclusions I couldn't prove, and letting anxiety cloud my trust. And yet, despite all of that, the Lord still reached out with kindness. He answered me through someone I least expected. That's the kind of grace I'll never forget.

## The Power of Scriptures in Times of Need

That morning, I had felt alone. But in reality, I was never alone.

It reminded me of Peter's experience in Matthew 14:28–32. He walks on water, but when he sees the storm around him, he became afraid and begins to sink. His cry is simple yet desperate: "Lord, save me!"[61]

And immediately, Jesus reaches out His hand and catches him.

I felt like Peter—overwhelmed, sinking in my worries. But at that moment, I was reminded that I was engraved on the palms of His hands.[62]

This is why scripture is so important. Elder Richard G. Scott once said that the scriptures "can become stalwart friends that are not limited by geography or calendar. They are always available when needed."[63]

The Holy Spirit will bring scriptures to our minds when we need them the most. The more we study and treasure them in our hearts, the more He can use them to whisper truth to us in difficult moments.

## Creating Perfect Moments in an Imperfect Life

Life isn't perfect. But as I once read online, "Life isn't perfect, but it has perfect moments." And I believe that one of the ways we can create those perfect moments is by turning to the scriptures.

---

61. Matthew 14:30.

62. Isaiah 49:16.

63. Richard G. Scott, *The Power of Scripture,* General Conference, Salt Lake City: The Church of Jesus Christ of Latter-day Saints, October 2001, Gospel Library App.

We can find small, intentional moments to bring scripture into our day:

- Lunchtime at work? Take five minutes to read a scripture and write down a few thoughts.
- Driving? Listen to the scriptures or a gospel podcast with one earbud while still being aware of your surroundings.
- Busy with family life? Keep a small notebook with spiritual topics you want to study next.

The important thing is to keep the scriptures close, to have a topic in mind that you want to learn more about.

When we always have a subject that we're seeking answers for, the scriptures become more than just pages of words—they become our best friends.

*Laís Gonçalves*

## Final Reflection: The Lord Never Leaves Us

Throughout my life, I have faced different struggles. Some have been small, like losing my keys and feeling anxious about what might happen. Others have been much heavier—grief, financial struggles, or spiritual challenges.

But no matter the trial, I have learned one thing with certainty: The Lord never leaves us.

Even when we feel like we are sinking, He is there. Even when we don't see Him, He is watching.

Because the truth is, He is always speaking. Sometimes, we just need to create the perfect moment to listen.

## Questions to Ponder

- When have I felt like I was sinking in my worries, and how did the Lord reach out to me during that time?
- How can I be more intentional about turning to scripture in my daily life so that I am spiritually prepared for moments of uncertainty?

- Do I truly believe that the Lord is aware of me in my struggles, and how can I strengthen my faith in His constant presence?
- What small yet meaningful actions can I take today to replace fear with faith and trust more fully in God's plan for me?

# 19

# Navigating Change and Uncertainty

## Trusting God's Plan During Transitions and Trials

IMMIGRATING TO ANOTHER COUNTRY IS NEVER EASY. WHILE OUR student visas provided stability for a time, there was always this quiet uncertainty in the background—the kind that makes you wonder, *What's next? What if things don't go as planned? Should we give up? Should we persevere?*

Before immigrating to the US, we had decided to always trust where the Lord would take us, even if it meant to go back to our home country soon after my husband completed his studies. That hasn't been the case so far.

For several years, our student visas allowed me to visit my family in Brazil at least once a year. Those visits were precious moments to reconnect with my grandparents, father, stepmother, and extended family. As someone who's always been deeply family-oriented, these visits mean everything to me.

But after Bruno graduated, that sense of uncertainty intensified. His student visa's OPT period—the temporary extension allowing international students to work—was coming to an end. For three consecutive years, Bruno entered the H-1B visa lottery—a highly competitive process administered by U.S. Citizenship and Immigration Services (USCIS), with only about a 25 percent chance of selection—and each year, he wasn't selected.

We trusted the Lord, but we knew faith couldn't replace action. We had been fasting weekly for four months, and yet nothing happened. We needed to keep moving forward. So, Bruno applied for a master's degree to maintain our legal status and give us more time. It was frustrating. We had been doing everything right, yet the opportunities we hoped for didn't seem to come, even when we felt this was where we needed to be.

## When Faith Requires Action

At one point, our immigration lawyer suggested another option: Since I had experience with my previous employer in Brazil, there was a possibility they could sponsor me for a position in the U.S. and support our application for permanent status.

We decided to move forward with this new option, trusting that the Lord would guide us. And He did. My former employer offered me a position, opening a new path toward visa stability.

But receiving their offer didn't mean everything was resolved. Securing that stability required months of submitting documents, waiting for approvals, and exchanging paperwork with USCIS. While we pursued this option through my employer, we also continued to hope and pray that Bruno would be selected for visa sponsorship through the company he worked for—uncertain which path, if any, would succeed.

Months passed. Bruno continued his studies, and we pressed forward, doing everything we could to stay prepared.

But as time stretched on, anxiety crept in, and with it, heartache. Because of our pending visa status, we couldn't leave the country without risking our ability to stay.

That meant missing moments that mattered deeply to me, moments I had always believed I'd be a part of.

I missed the weddings of two cousins, people I had grown up with, laughed with, and shared memories with. One of them lived with us for a time in Rexburg, Idaho, to learn English. She felt like a little sister to me. Missing her wedding felt like missing part of my own family story.

I also missed my sweet niece's baptism, her special day of covenant-making, and my grandfather's funeral, whom I could've visited at the hospital, months prior. That broke my heart most of all.

The hardest part wasn't just missing these moments, it was the helplessness. I felt like my hands were tied and there was nothing I could do.

Still, despite the uncertainty and disappointment, there was peace—a quiet, steady reassurance that the Lord was in control.

## The Miracle in God's Timing

As Bruno's master's program neared its end, we felt the pressure mounting again. What if we reached the end of this degree and still had no way to stay?

But just as the first week of his final semester approached, we received unexpected news—the kind that brings instant relief.

Our work permit arrived.

This permit allowed both Bruno and me to work in the U.S. without needing a student visa. For the first time, we no longer had to worry about our visa status. We were overwhelmed with gratitude—but God's blessings didn't stop there

Shortly after, Bruno's company contacted him with incredible news: after years of applying and never being selected, his name had finally been drawn in the visa lottery.

At that moment, we knew: the Lord had been preparing the way all along.

Had Bruno's visa had been granted earlier, he likely would have left his master's program unfinished—missing out on the knowledge, experience, and growth that degree brought. But because of the delay, Bruno completed his degree. Today, that additional education has opened new doors. He now balances his career with something he loves deeply: teaching at Ensign College.

Looking back, I can see that the Lord had a purpose in every delay. What once felt like a series of obstacles was actually a carefully designed path—one that led to greater opportunities, deeper growth, and unexpected blessings.

## Lessons from the Waiting

This experience taught me that trusting the Lord isn't just about believing. It's about continuing to act in faith, even when answers don't come right away.

"For ye receive no witness until after the trial of your faith."[64]

We didn't receive immediate answers, but we moved forward in faith. Bruno kept studying while working full-time. I kept doing what I could to ease that burden. We trusted that God would provide, and He did—not just with what we hoped for, but with something far greater.

It was a quiet, humbling confirmation that everything had unfolded exactly as the Lord intended. Had we been chosen earlier, we might have stepped away from opportunities that ended up shaping Bruno's path and our future. We had done everything we could—with faith, fasting, and sacrifice—but in the end, it was the Lord's timing that prevailed.

I've learned that God's timing often looks different from ours. What feels like a frustrating delay may be a carefully placed detour—one that leads to experiences, growth, and blessings we wouldn't have seen otherwise.

If you're facing uncertainty, waiting for answers that don't seem to come, I invite you to hold on. Keep praying. Keep working. Keep trusting. Keep moving.

Because when you put your faith in God's timing, you'll find that He's been preparing the way all along.

"Be still, and know that I am God."[65]

*Leticia Araujo*

---

64. Ether 12:6.

65. Psalm 46:10.

## Questions to Ponder

Life rarely unfolds exactly the way we plan. At times the delays, detours, or disappointments we experience feel overwhelming. But I've learned those moments can become some of the greatest evidence of God's hand in our lives.

I invite you to reflect on your own journey:

- **Can you recall a time when God's timing didn't match your expectations, yet looking back, you could see His hand guiding you?** Consider how that experience may have shaped you or prepared you for something greater.
- **What helps you hold on to faith when answers seem delayed or unclear?** Are there scriptures, prayers, or spiritual practices that give you strength in those waiting seasons?
- **Have you ever faced a closed door or unexpected detour in life?** How did you choose to move forward in faith? What gave you the courage to trust that God had a plan?
- **How can you better recognize God's peace, even when your circumstances feel uncertain?** Reflect on moments when the Lord's quiet reassurance calmed your fears, even when solutions hadn't yet arrived.
- **What experiences in your life once felt disappointing, but now you can see they were part of God's greater plan?** How did those experiences—painful as they may have been—prepare you for future blessings?

As you ponder these questions, I encourage you to look for the patterns in your life where God's unseen hand was guiding you all along. Sometimes the answers we seek are already unfolding—quietly, patiently—right before our eyes.

# 20
# Healing Through Forgiveness

Forgiveness isn't just a commandment; it's a divine gift that brings healing, peace, and freedom. Jesus Christ is the ultimate example of forgiveness. From the cross, He utters the profound words: "Father, forgive them; for they know not what they do" (Luke 23:34). If the Son of God forgives those who crucified Him, surely, we can learn to forgive those who have wronged us.

That said, forgiveness isn't always easy—especially when the wounds run deep. But through Christ's Atonement, we can find the strength to let go of resentment and embrace peace. Modern psychology backs this up, too. Studies show that forgiveness leads to lower anxiety, less depression, and even reduced chronic pain.[66] Who knew the scriptures had been onto something this whole time?

66. *Forgiveness Your Health Depends on It.* Hopkins Medicine. https://www.hopkinsmedicine.org/health/wellness-and-prevention/forgiveness-your-health-depends-on-it; Sheena O'Beirne, Anna-Maria Katsimigos, and Dominic Harmon, *Forgiveness and chronic pain: a systematic review,* National Library of Medicine, 2020 Nov 189(4) 1359-1364, www.doi.org/10.1007/s11845-020-02200-y.

It's important that we all learn how forgiveness can mend our souls, restore inner peace, and help us fully embrace Christ's healing power.

## Step 1: Recognize the Need for Healing Through Forgiveness

President Gordon B. Hinckley once said: "If there be any within the sound of my voice who nurture in their hearts the poisonous brew of enmity toward another, I plead with you to ask the Lord for strength to forgive."[67]

Holding onto grudges is like carrying around a backpack full of bricks: It's exhausting, unnecessary, and honestly, not a great look. I know this from personal experience.

A few years ago, I struggled to forgive someone, and after nearly two years, the pain and resentment were turning me into a person I didn't want to be. Then, during a stake conference, the stake president shared a story that changed my perspective.

He told of a group of young people who went on a picnic in the desert. As you probably know, desert landscapes aren't exactly lush—mostly mesquite, catclaw, palo verde trees, and the occasional cactus. And, of course, rattlesnakes.

While playing, one girl got bitten by a rattlesnake. At that moment, the group had two options:

- Immediately tend to her wound, extracting the venom before it spread
- Chase down the snake and make sure it never bit anyone again

Unfortunately, they chose option #2. They ran after the snake, throwing rocks until they finally killed it. Only then did they remember their injured friend. But by that time, the venom had traveled deep into her bloodstream. She made it to the hospital, but the delay had caused severe tissue damage, and doctors had to amputate her leg

67. Gordon B. Hinckley, *Of You It Is Required to Forgive*, General Conference (Salt Lake City: The Church of Jesus Christ of Latter-day Saints), October 1980, Gospel Library App.

below the knee to save her life. The stake president then compared rattlesnake venom to holding a grudge.

When we refuse to forgive, we allow the poison of resentment to spread, harming our spiritual and emotional well-being. We get so focused on making sure the other person "pays" that we forget about our own healing.

That story hit me hard. I realized that forgiveness isn't about letting someone off the hook; it's about getting rid of the poison in our own souls. When we let go of anger, we make room for healing.

## Step 2: Seek the Savior's Healing Power

Joseph Smith endured betrayal and false accusations, yet he counseled the Saints to rely on the Lord: "Let us cheerfully do all things that lie in our power; and then may we stand still, with the utmost assurance, to see the salvation of God."[68]

At some point in our lives, we all experience hurt. Sometimes it's a minor offense that stings for a moment, like a rude comment or a thoughtless act. Other times, the wounds cut deep—betrayal, abandonment, or cruelty that shakes us to our core. In those moments, forgiveness can feel impossible. But the Atonement of Jesus Christ is designed for moments just like these.

The Savior's sacrifice wasn't just about overcoming sin, but about healing broken hearts. In Luke 4:18, Christ declares: "He hath sent me to heal the brokenhearted, to preach deliverance to the captives, and recovering of sight to the blind, to set at liberty them that are bruised."

Notice that? Healing. Deliverance. Liberation. That's what the Atonement is about. It is for the bruised, the broken, and the burdened—for those weighed down by sorrow, pain, and yes, even resentment.

When we think of the Atonement, we often focus on repentance—the power to be cleansed from sin. But it's also the greatest source of healing in our lives. The Atonement doesn't just make bad people good; it makes wounded people whole.

---

68. Doctrine and Covenants 123:17.

The prophet Alma describes this healing power beautifully when he prophesies of Christ:

"And he shall go forth, suffering pains and afflictions and temptations of every kind; and this that the word might be fulfilled which saith he will take upon him the pains and the sicknesses of his people . . . that he may know according to the flesh how to succor his people."[69]

Christ understands every pain we carry—not just our sins, but our grief, our heartache, our loneliness, and our anger. He feels every betrayal, every insult, every moment of heartache that has ever existed. Because of that, He knows how to comfort us perfectly.

When we struggle to forgive, we can turn to Him—not just to ask for help, but to receive healing. Sometimes, we don't forgive because we don't know *how*. The pain is too fresh. The injustice feels too great. But Jesus doesn't expect us to do this alone. That's why He invites us:

"Come unto me, all ye that labour and are heavy laden, and I will give you rest."[70]

Forgiveness isn't just about letting go of the offense—it's about allowing Christ to carry the burden for us.

One of the most beautiful miracles of the Atonement is how it changes us from the inside out. The more we come unto Christ, the more our hearts soften.

Doctrine and Covenants 98 teaches us that forgiveness isn't a one-time act, but a process: "Thou shalt forgive him unto seventy times seven."[71]

Sound familiar? That's a direct reference to Matthew 18:22, when Peter asked Jesus how often he should forgive. Christ's response—"Until seventy times seven"—isn't meant to be a literal number. He is teaching that forgiveness is a process we return to as many times as it takes.

There are times when forgiveness doesn't happen overnight. Sometimes, we have to forgive again and again, layer by layer, piece by piece.

---

69. Alma 7:11–12.

70. Matthew 11:28.

71. Doctrine and Covenants 98:40.

That's where the Atonement comes in.

Through Christ, we can take our wounds, our bitterness, our resentment and lay them at His feet. We don't have to carry the hurt forever. He will heal us, soften our hearts, and make it possible to move forward.

One day, while I was still struggling with that same person from the snake poison story, I sought comfort in the temple. I wanted peace, but I wasn't sure how to get there. I prayed and asked for guidance. That's when I miraculously opened to Doctrine and Covenants 98:44–45 and read the scripture in the celestial room:

> But if he trespass against thee the fourth time thou shalt not forgive him, but shalt bring these testimonies before the Lord; and they shall not be blotted out until he repent and reward thee four-fold in all things wherewith he has trespassed against thee. And if he do this, thou shalt forgive him with all thine heart; and if he do not this, I, the Lord, will avenge thee of thine enemy an hundred-fold.

At first, I was taken aback—wasn't this contradicting the idea of always forgiving? But as I read more, a realization struck me: The most important part of this scripture wasn't about vengeance. It was about the instruction to bring these testimonies before the Lord.

I realized that I didn't have to carry this burden alone. Instead of holding onto pain, I could lay it all before Christ—my hurt, my frustration, my suffering.

I remember physically visualizing this moment—lifting my hands as if offering a small box filled with my burdens to the Savior. *Lord, I have done all I can. I give this to You.* And in that moment, I felt peace.

Did the relationship magically fix itself? No. Did the hurt immediately disappear? Not completely. But I felt lighter. I felt free. And from that day on, I knew—no matter what was said or done—the Lord was aware.

He would take care of me. He would provide justice. And that was enough.

The Atonement of Jesus Christ has real power—not just to cleanse us, but to heal us. When we struggle to forgive, when the pain seems too much, when we don't know how to move forward—we can turn to Him.

## Step 3: Choose to Let Go and Allow Healing to Begin

Forgiveness is not passive; it's a choice. It's something we have to decide, sometimes daily, sometimes hourly, until our hearts fully release the weight of resentment.

But honestly, sometimes, choosing to forgive feels impossible. Our emotions don't always cooperate with what we know we should do.

When someone has deeply hurt us, our instinct is to hold onto the pain as a form of self-protection. We think:

- *If I forgive them, they'll think what they did was okay*
- *If I let this go, they'll never understand how much they hurt me*
- *They don't deserve my forgiveness*

Sound familiar? The problem is, holding onto resentment doesn't protect us—it poisons us.

There's a saying that holding a grudge is like drinking poison and expecting the other person to die. The more we clutch onto bitterness, the more it consumes us. Meanwhile, the person who hurt us? They might not even realize the depth of our pain. Or worse—they might not care. But that's exactly why forgiveness is about freeing ourselves, not them.

Few people in scripture have as many reasons to hold a grudge as Nephi. From the very beginning, his older brothers, Laman and Lemuel, make his life difficult. They murmur against him. They mock him. They tie him up and even try to kill him—multiple times.

Nephi has every right to feel angry. He could choose to spend his life dwelling on their cruelty. But instead, he chooses to forgive.

In 1 Nephi 7:16, Laman and Lemuel tie up Nephi and leave him in the wilderness to die. But instead of plotting revenge, Nephi prays for deliverance—and the Lord strengthens him to break free. Later, in 1 Nephi 17:48, when his brothers threaten to kill him again, he responds with faith, calling upon the Lord's power to protect him.

Even after everything, Nephi continues to love and forgive his brothers. He prays for them. He wants them to change. He doesn't let their actions turn him into someone bitter or hateful.

However, there came a point when Nephi has to step away for his own safety. In 2 Nephi 5:5, the Lord warns him: "And it came to pass that the Lord did warn me, that I, Nephi, should depart from them and flee into the wilderness, and all those who would go with me."

Nephi's story teaches us an important truth:

- Forgiving does not mean allowing someone to keep hurting us
- Forgiving does not mean staying in a toxic situation
- Forgiving does mean trusting God and choosing peace

Nephi's decision to separate from his brothers isn't out of hatred—but out of obedience to the Lord. He moves forward, builds a new life, and continues to serve God with faith.

Letting go isn't easy. Some wounds run deep. Some betrayals change the course of our lives. And in those moments, forgiveness doesn't just feel difficult—it feels unfair.

That's when we have to remember: Forgiveness isn't something we do on our own. It's something we do through Christ.

When our hearts feel hardened, we can pray: *Lord, I want to forgive, but I don't know how. Please help me let go.*

Even if we don't feel like we can forgive right now, we can ask Him to change our hearts. Over time, He will.

Forgiveness isn't a one-time decision. Sometimes, we forgive only to feel the anger creeping back in days, weeks, or even years later. That's okay.

It's a process.

It means we choose peace over pain.

It means we trust God more than the comfort of our anger.

It means we let Christ heal what we cannot heal on our own.

## Step 4: Act in Love and Service to Deepen Inner Healing

Jesus doesn't just say "forgive your enemies" and leave it at that; He takes it a step further: "Love your enemies, bless them that curse you, do good to them that hate you, and pray for them which despitefully use you."[72]

72. Matthew 5:44.

That's . . . a tall order, but incredibly powerful. Modern psychology backs this up with practices like loving-kindness meditation, which helps cultivate compassion for even the most difficult people.

A simple version of this practice goes like this:

- Start by saying: "May I be happy. May I be free from suffering. May I be at peace."
- Then extend that to others, including the person who hurt you: "May they find peace. May they learn from their mistakes. May I let go of this pain."

It might feel weird at first, but over time, it softens the edges of resentment and helps us move forward. If this type of meditation doesn't resonate with you, start by praying for that person. The prayer might feel insincere. (It sure did for me.) But as we allow ourselves to speak kindly of them that hurt us, healing starts to come as we let go of the negativity.

## Step 5: Trust in Divine Justice and Find Peace

One of the hardest parts of forgiveness is letting go of the idea that justice must be served. When we've been wronged, it's natural to think, *But what if they never pay for what they did?* The truth is, justice will come—but that's not where our focus should be.

If we hold too tightly to the idea of justice, we risk turning forgiveness into a waiting game—one where we don't feel at peace until we see consequences. That's not healing; that's bitterness disguised as patience.

In Alma 14, Alma and Amulek watch as innocent believers are burned alive. Devastated, Amulek asks Alma if they should stop it. Alma, with great faith, replies: "The Spirit constraineth me that I must not stretch forth mine hand; for behold, the Lord receiveth them up unto himself, in glory."[73]

Alma understands that justice isn't his to carry. Eventually, Ammonihah is destroyed[74], but Alma and Amulek don't wait around for it.

---

73. Alma 14:11.

74. Alma 16:9–10.

They move forward. They continue preaching, serving, and trusting God. They do not let vengeance take up space in their hearts.

Doctrine and Covenants 64:9–10 teaches: "Wherefore, I say unto you, that ye ought to forgive one another; for he that forgiveth not his brother his trespasses standeth condemned before the Lord . . . I, the Lord, will forgive whom I will forgive, but of you it is required to forgive all men."

Notice that the Lord says *He will forgive whom He will forgive.* It's not our job. If we take it upon ourselves to act as judge, jury, and executioner—even in our own minds—we risk condemning ourselves in the process.

The Lord has promised that He will right every wrong. The challenge for us is to let go of the need to see it happen.

I found this quote online: "When it comes to our own sins, we want mercy. But when it comes to the sins of others, we demand justice."[75]

Ouch.

It's easy to want justice for others and mercy for ourselves. But what if God holds us to that same standard?

Think about all the times we have messed up. The things we've said that hurt others. The mistakes we wish we could take back.

If we expect mercy from God, we must be willing to extend it to others.

This is why trusting in divine justice comes last. If we focus on it too much, we may never truly forgive. We may walk around clinging to the hope that we'll one day witness the downfall of those who have hurt us.

That isn't peace. That isn't healing. That isn't forgiveness.

Forgiveness is:

- Choosing peace over resentment
- Letting go, even when there's no closure
- Trusting that God sees everything and will handle it in His own way

---

75. Unknown Author.

And most importantly, forgiveness is about us, not them. It's about our freedom, our healing, and our happiness.

The Lord's justice will come, but we don't need to wait for it. We don't need to expect it. We don't even need to think about it.

Forgiveness isn't easy, but it is worth it. It takes strength to release anger, faith to let go of justice, and humility to trust God with the outcome. But as we do, we step into something far greater than the pain of the past. We step into Christ's love.

So, let us lay down our burdens at His feet. Let us release what is holding us back. Let us stop drinking the poison of bitterness and instead drink deeply from the well of healing and grace.

At the end of the day, we don't forgive because they deserve it; we forgive because we deserve peace. And that peace is exactly what Christ is offering us.

*Ana Castro*

## Questions to Ponder

- What is one past hurt or offense that I still hold onto? How has it affected my emotional and spiritual well-being?
- When I think about forgiving someone, what emotions come up? What fears or concerns do I have about letting go?
- How have I experienced the healing power of the Atonement in my life? In what ways can I rely on Christ more fully to help me forgive?
- Do I secretly hold onto the expectation of justice or an apology before I feel ready to forgive? How might this be keeping me from truly healing?
- Nephi forgave his brothers repeatedly, yet he also knew when it was time to walk away. Are there any relationships in my life where I need to set healthy boundaries while still choosing to forgive?
- When I think about someone who has hurt me, do I focus more on their wrong doing or on how I can heal? How can I shift my perspective toward Christ and personal peace?

# Part VI

# Deepening Spiritual Practices

# 21

# Prayer: Connecting Through Scripture

## Enriching Your Prayers with Scriptural Passages

PRAYER HAS LONG BEEN A LIFELINE FOR ME, A VITAL CONNECTION TO my Heavenly Father in moments of joy, struggle, and growth. Honestly, between taking care of kids, meeting work deadlines, fulfilling Church callings, trying to make it to the temple, running a podcast (which, let me tell you, is *way* more work than it seems), and all the other things constantly demanding my attention, prayer can sometimes take a backseat. It's all too easy to let prayer slip into the background, a fleeting thought instead of a meaningful conversation with my Father in Heaven.

As part of a semester-long project in my online Doctrine and Covenants class at BYU–Idaho, each student was invited to choose a gospel principle to study, set goals around, and live more fully for eleven weeks. I chose prayer.

Now, don't get me wrong—I *knew* prayer was important. I mean, I grew up learning that. But I had to admit, my consistency wasn't great. Life just had a way of crowding out those quiet moments I desperately needed to connect with my Father in Heaven.

During my studies, I came across a talk by President James E. Faust, "The Lifeline of Prayer," from the April 2002 general conference. The title alone opened my eyes. I asked my good old friend, ChatGPT, what a lifeline was, and this was the response I got:

> A lifeline is something that provides crucial support or help in times of need, offering a means of rescue, stability, or guidance during challenging situations. Literally, it can refer to a rope used for saving lives, such as in emergencies at sea. Metaphorically, it represents anything that sustains or aids someone in difficulty, like emotional support, financial assistance, or critical resources.

Okay, first of all, that definition was way more profound than I expected. Second, the words that jumped out at me? *Rescue, stability, and guidance.*

As I navigate a divorce right now, those words hit *deep.* That's exactly what I need—rescue, stability, and guidance. And I've realized that prayer is the key to all three.

## PRAYER AS RESCUE

The story of Alma the Younger in the Book of Mormon powerfully illustrates how prayer can rescue us from the depths of despair and sin. In Alma 36, Alma recounts his experience of profound sorrow for his rebellion against God. In verses 18–20, we read:

> Now, as my mind caught hold upon this thought, I cried within my heart: O Jesus, thou Son of God, have mercy on me, who am in the gall of bitterness, and am encircled about by the everlasting chains of death. And now, behold, when I thought this, I could remember my pains no more; yea, I was harrowed up by the memory of my sins no more. And oh, what joy, and what marvelous light I did behold; yea, my soul was filled with joy as exceeding as was my pain!

In Alma's darkest hour, his heartfelt plea to God became his lifeline. That prayer not only rescues him from spiritual anguish but allows him to experience the transformative power of the Savior's Atonement.

Similarly, I found myself relying on prayer as a source of rescue. During moments when grief and anger threatened to overwhelm me, I learned that earnest prayer could lift my soul and remind me of the Savior's love and healing power.

President James E. Faust described prayer as a "humble earnest petition addressed to God." That word *earnest* really sticks with me. When we're at our lowest, real prayer isn't polished or perfect. It's raw. It's messy. And that's okay, because prayer isn't about getting the words right. It's about being vulnerable and admitting we need divine help. It's about being humble enough to allow Him to rescue us.

## Prayer as Stability

Now, how does prayer bring stability? This made me think of anchors, and how they can be viewed as a lifeline for a boat. If a boat is not anchored, it wanders into dangerous waters. But when anchored, it is stable. Yes, it will move a little here and there, but it will not wander and get lost. Prayer brings us stability because it grounds us and connects us to our Heavenly Father. We may be in the middle of rough, choppy, dangerous waters, but we will not wander. We are stable in our beliefs and in our trust that God will provide a way to safety.

In my own life, when I have been able to pray consistently every day and every night, I found a sense of stability. The waves crashing around me didn't disappear, but I was at peace and comforted by the knowledge and faith I had in my Savior and Heavenly Father. I felt an inner calm that enabled me to keep moving forward. Constant prayer did that for me. It kept me grounded when everything else felt unpredictable and impossible to control. But He was in control. There's no better example of this than Joseph Smith in Liberty Jail.

He was unjustly jailed. He was suffering. His family was suffering. His friends were suffering. I can only imagine how dark of a place his mind must have gone to while in Liberty Jail. Section 121 of the Doctrine and Covenants gives us a glimpse of how he might have been feeling, alone and forgotten. This section is a heartfelt prayer from Joseph to God and a loving response from a loving Savior. In verse 7–8, the Lord says, "My son, peace be unto thy soul; thine adversity and thine afflictions shall be but a small moment; And then, if thou endure it well, God shall exalt thee on high; thou shalt triumph over all thy foes."

While this did not change Joseph's circumstances, he was given peace. He received inner strength to carry on, but most of all he received confirmation that the Lord was aware of His faithful servant, that He was in control, and that He would bring Joseph to eternal safety, peace, and stability.

Like Joseph, I've learned that consistent, heartfelt prayer provides stability even amid life's storms. While the waves may still crash around me, I feel grounded knowing that my Heavenly Father is guiding my path. This brings to mind the powerful story of Jesus calming the storm. In Mark 4:37–39, we read:

> And there arose a great storm of wind, and the waves beat into the ship, so that it was now full. And he was in the hinder part of the ship, asleep on a pillow: and they awake him, and say unto him, Master, carest thou not that we perish? And he arose, and rebuked the wind, and said unto the sea, Peace, be still. And the wind ceased, and there was a great calm.

This miracle demonstrates the Savior's power to bring peace and stability, even in the midst of literal and figurative storms. When we turn to Him in prayer, He can calm the turbulent waters in our lives. He may not necessarily remove the trial, ache, or tribulation we are facing, but He will calm our spirits and help us to feel peace. His gentle command, "Peace, be still," can fill our hearts as we seek His help, reminding us that He is always near, ready to bring calm and clarity.

## Prayer as Guidance

One of my favorite stories in the scriptures is when Nephi is told to build a ship. Can we just take a moment to appreciate how wild that must have been?

Nephi isn't a shipbuilder. He has no clue how to do it. But he goes to the Lord, and the Lord gives him step-by-step guidance.

In 1 Nephi 17:7–8, Nephi recounts being instructed by the Lord: "Arise, and get thee into the mountain. And it came to pass that I arose and went up into the mountain, and cried unto the Lord. And it came to pass that the Lord spake unto me, saying: Thou shalt construct a ship, after the manner which I shall show thee."

Nephi's willingness to seek the Lord's guidance and follow His instructions leads to the deliverance of his family.

While I've never received such detailed instructions in my prayers, I've experienced the Lord's guidance in deeply personal ways. One of my goals during my project on prayer was to take time to ponder after praying. Though moments of stillness are rare as a busy mother, I found sacred opportunities to listen for the Lord's voice, particularly in the temple. On one occasion, as I prayed about a difficult co-parenting moment, I felt inspired to open the scriptures. The verses I read were exactly what I needed and provided clear guidance for my situation. That moment reaffirmed to me that God speaks to us when we seek Him with real intent.

Guidance through prayer is not always immediate or obvious. Sometimes it comes as a quiet prompting, a thought that lingers in our mind, or a feeling of peace that reassures us we are on the right path. Other times, it comes through the words of scripture, a talk from a Church leader, or the counsel of a trusted friend. I've learned that the key is to be patient and to trust that the Lord's timing and wisdom are perfect.

One of the most profound lessons I've learned is the power of combining prayer with scripture study. The scriptures often provide the answers, comfort, and insights we seek in prayer. As Elder Richard G. Scott taught, "Scriptures are like packets of light that illuminate our minds and give place to guidance and inspiration from on high."[76]

I've made it a habit to keep my scriptures close when I pray, especially during times of personal reflection. Often, I'll begin with a prayer, asking for guidance or clarity on a specific question or concern. Then, as I open the scriptures, I'll find verses that speak directly to my heart. These moments remind me that God knows me personally and that He is eager to communicate with me through His word.

One of my favorite scriptures is Ether 12:27, which reads: "And if men come unto me I will show unto them their weakness."

---

76. Richard G. Scott, *The Power of Scripture*, General Conference (Salt Lake City: The Church of Jesus Christ of Latter-day Saints), October 2011, Gospel Library App.

This verse is a profound reminder that when we approach our Heavenly Father in sincere prayer, He will lovingly open our eyes to areas where we need to grow. These weaknesses might be personal flaws, sins we struggle with, or blind spots in our perspective. For instance, we may be facing a challenge in our relationships—be it with a friend, spouse, or coworker. In these situations, we might feel justified in our stance, believing we are right and holding our ground. Yet through prayer, Heavenly Father can expand our understanding. He may help us see the situation from a new angle, allowing us to develop compassion and empathy for the other person. This shift in perspective paves the way for a resolution that aligns with gospel principles while preserving our integrity.

Coming to the Lord in humility allows Him to show us the bigger picture. Sometimes, the insights we gain are less about changing the external situation and more about changing our hearts. Whether He grants us wisdom to approach a conflict with grace, or strengthens us to endure challenges with faith, prayer becomes a channel through which He empowers us to move forward confidently, always trusting in His divine support.

Life does require a lot from us. As Latter-day Saint women, we juggle so many things—our families, our responsibilities, our personal growth, and everything in between. Prayer is what makes it all possible. It connects us to our Heavenly Father, reminds us of our divine worth, and gives us the strength and guidance we need to handle whatever comes our way.

Prayer isn't just another item to check off the to-do list; it's a lifeline to our Heavenly Father. Through prayer, I've felt His rescue in moments of despair, His anchor in the middle of chaos, and His guidance when I've needed it most. When we combine prayer with scripture study, it strengthens that connection even more, helping us find answers and peace.

So, if you're feeling overwhelmed (or let's be honest, even if you're not), I invite you to make prayer a priority. Not just the rushed, half-asleep kind (been there), but the kind that pulls you closer to God.

Because I promise—He's listening. He always has been. And He always will be.

*Ana de Castro*

## Questions to Ponder

- Reflect on a time in your life when you felt overwhelmed, lost, or in need of divine help. How did turning to prayer bring you relief or clarity? If you are currently in a difficult season, what specific burdens can you take to the Lord in prayer today?
- Consider your current prayer habits. Do you feel anchored in your relationship with God, or do life's distractions often pull you away from meaningful prayer? What small changes can you make to ensure prayer is a consistent source of stability in your daily life?
- Think about a time when you felt inspired or received personal revelation through prayer. How did that experience shape your decisions or strengthen your testimony? What are some ways you can create space in your life to listen for God's guidance more intentionally?

# 22

# Meditating on God's Word

## Developing the Habit of Reflective Study and Application

When I first read the Book of Mormon cover to cover, I was fourteen years old. This marked a turning point in my spiritual life. It was the first time I truly engaged with the scriptures. I had just started seminary and felt a growing desire to deepen my understanding of God's teachings. In the past, I had read passages here and there, but this time was different. This time, I wasn't simply reading for information; I was reading with a yearning to connect, to know God more personally, and to feel the power of His word.

Every day after school, I would eat lunch, then retreat upstairs to read. My special spot was a blue hammock chair on the "laje," the rooftop balcony of our house. The *sobrado*—similar to a town home in the U.S.—had a narrow corridor to the master bedroom's balcony extended over the garage. My mother had covered half of it, installing the hammock securely to the ceiling. It became my sanctuary.

I remember the warmth of the sun on my skin, the gentle breeze that carried the sounds of the neighborhood, and the profound peace that filled me as I pondered the words I had just read. It was in that hammock, in the stillness of the afternoon, that I first began to meditate on God's word. For the first time, I wasn't just reading; I was reflecting. I was allowing those sacred words to enter my heart and transform my thoughts.

## From Distraction to Dedication: The Challenge of Meditation in Busy Life

As life grew busier, I struggled to maintain the same peaceful routine. The demands of work, school, and other responsibilities made it harder to find time for quiet reflection. I started working and attending college, which meant my schedule was relentless. My day would start at 6 a.m. when I'd catch the bus for my one-hour commute to work in São Paulo South. After work, I had another hour-long commute to college, and then a 30-minute trip back home late at night. I would get home between 11:00 and midnight. Between the noise and exhaustion, finding quiet moments for scripture study seemed nearly impossible.

But I quickly discovered that even amid chaos, moments of peace could still be found. I found solace in those long commuting hours. Sitting on the bus, surrounded by the noise of the city, I would open my scriptures and meditate on the Lord's words. Those precious moments of reflection turned my tiring, chaotic days into more peaceful, centered ones. The practice of meditation became my anchor, grounding me in the midst of a busy life.

It was a practice that didn't need to take place at a specific time or location. Life is unpredictable, and while early mornings can offer a sense of tranquility, there are many times when peace can only be found in the midst of a busy schedule. Meditation can be done during a commute, a lunch break, or even before bed. The key isn't the time or place—it's the intention to create space in your heart and mind to focus on God.

Joshua 1:8 teaches us: "This book of the law shall not depart out of thy mouth; but thou shalt meditate therein day and night." Meditation isn't simply about thinking; it's about internalizing God's word so that it becomes part of who we are. As we meditate, we give God room to speak to our hearts, to shape our thoughts, and to align our will with His.

## The Power of Meditation: Connecting with God Through Reflection

Meditation isn't just an intellectual exercise. I t's an opportunity to connect with God on a deeper level. It allows us to quiet our minds and create a space for God's Spirit to fill. The act of meditating on God's word helps us to slow down, reflect, and listen. It's an invitation to surrender our own understanding and be open to revelation.

Sometimes, we may feel as if we're seeking answers from God but are met with silence. This can be one of the most difficult aspects of our spiritual journey—especially when we want answers right away. In these moments, meditation becomes a vital practice. Rather than striving for immediate clarity, we can create a sacred space where we allow God to speak to us in His own time. This requires patience and trust.

The story of Elijah on Mount Horeb is a powerful example of how revelation often comes: "And after the earthquake a fire; but the Lord was not in the fire: and after the fire a still small voice."[77] Elijah's experience shows us that revelation doesn't always come with a dramatic display. Sometimes, it is quiet, subtle, and deeply personal. We need to train our hearts and minds to recognize God's voice in the stillness.

As Elder David A. Bednar taught: "Revelation often comes as small and incremental impressions that are facilitated by pondering, prayer, and consistent obedience."[78] This reinforces the idea that meditation doesn't just prepare us for spiritual moments; it cultivates the kind of spiritual sensitivity that allows us to recognize God's guidance in everyday life.

## How to Begin Meditating on God's Word

If you are new to meditation, or if you've struggled to make it a consistent practice, don't be discouraged. Meditation is a habit that can be developed with intention and patience. Here are some simple steps you can take to start meditating on God's word:

---

77. 1 Kings 19:12.

78. David A. Bednar, *The Spirit of Revelation,* General Conference (Salt Lake City: The Church of Jesus Christ of Latter-day Saints), Apr. 2011, Gospel Library App.

1. **Choose a Scripture Passage**: Select a verse or chapter that resonates with you. It could be a passage that you've read before or something that feels particularly relevant to your life right now.
2. **Find a Quiet Space**: A quiet space helps create an environment conducive to reflection. This could be in a room at home, a park, or even in your car. The key is to eliminate distractions and focus on God.
3. **Read Slowly and Reflect**: Read the passage slowly. Pause after each sentence or phrase, allowing the meaning to sink in. Read it multiple times if needed, focusing on different words or phrases each time.
4. **Pray for Understanding**: Ask God to help you understand the message He wants to convey to you through this scripture. Pray for clarity and insight.
5. **Listen and Write**: As you meditate, listen for the Spirit's impressions. Write down any thoughts, feelings, or insights that come to you. Sometimes, the act of writing can help solidify these spiritual impressions.
6. **Apply the Message**: After you reflect on the passage, think about how you can live out its message in your daily life. Meditating on God's word isn't just about understanding it; it's about applying it.

## A Guided Meditation: Five Minutes of Reflection

If you're new to meditation, or if you want to deepen your practice, here is a simple guided meditation to help you connect with God:

- **Setting the Atmosphere**—Find a comfortable, quiet place. Dim the lights or sit in natural sunlight. Take a few deep breaths and release any distractions. Allow yourself to settle into the moment.
- **Step 1: Slow Down (1 minute)**—Take a few deep breaths. With each inhale, imagine drawing in God's peace. With each exhale, release any worries or stress. Allow your body and mind to relax.

- **Step 2: Read and Reflect (2 minutes)**—Choose a scripture, such as Psalm 46:10: "Be still, and know that I am God." Read it slowly and thoughtfully. Let each word settle into your heart. What stands out to you? What does God want you to learn from this verse today?
- **Step 3: Listen for God's Voice (1 minute)**—Close your eyes and silently ask God, "What do You want me to learn from this verse today?" Sit in stillness and allow His Spirit to whisper to your heart. Trust that He will guide you.
- **Step 4: Commit to Action (1 minute)**—Write down one small way you can apply this scripture today. It could be showing kindness, trusting in a difficult situation, or simply choosing gratitude. Make a commitment to act on the inspiration you've received.

## The Impact of Meditation on Spiritual and Emotional Healing

Meditating on God's word doesn't only deepen our faith, it also brings healing to our hearts and minds. Scientific research has shown that mindfulness and meditation can reduce stress, anxiety, and even physical pain. Studies also suggest that meditation increases emotional resilience and mental clarity, which makes it easier to handle life's challenges.

For example, a study by Harvard Medical School[79] found that mindfulness meditation increased gray matter in the hippocampus, the part of the brain that helps with learning, memory, and emotional regulation. In other words, taking time to slow down and be still doesn't just feel good—it physically strengthens the parts of your brain that help you think clearly and manage stress. This makes meditation not just a spiritual tool, but a powerful act of self-care for mental and emotional resilience.

79. Britta K. Holzel, James Carmody, Mark Vangel, Christina Congleton, Sita M. Yerramsetti, Tim Gard, & Sara W. Lazar, "Mindfulness Practice Leads to Increases in Regional Brain Gray Matter Density," *Psychiatry Research: Neuroimaging,* 191(1), 36–43, https://doi.org/10.1016/j.pscychresns.2010.08.006.

In addition, a 2014 study published in *JAMA Internal Medicine*[80] found that mindfulness meditation can significantly reduce symptoms of anxiety, depression, and stress—effects comparable to antidepressants. This resonates with the message in the scriptures that meditation on God's word brings peace to the soul. Jesus said in John 14:27, "Peace I leave with you, my peace I give unto you: not as the world giveth, give I unto you."

## The Joy of a Meditative Life

Developing the habit of meditating on God's word is one of the most powerful ways to strengthen our spiritual foundation. It isn't about perfection; it's about presence. The goal is to create space in our lives where God can speak to us, where we can listen and receive His peace.

I invite you to commit to just five minutes a day. Choose a verse, reflect, listen, and apply. Watch as your connection with God grows, your spirit heals, and your faith flourishes. God is waiting to meet you in the stillness. The more you meditate on His word, the more you will feel His presence and guidance in your life.

*Caroline Melazzo*

## Questions to Ponder

- How do you currently make time to meditate on God's word? How might you create more space in your life for this practice?
- Think about a time when you received an impression or answer through meditation. How did it affect your life?
- In what ways can you make meditation a consistent part of your spiritual journey, even in the midst of a busy life?

80. Madhav Goyal, Sonal Singh, Erica M. S. Sibinga, Neda F. Gould, Anastasia Rowland-Seymour, Ritu Sharma, Zackary Berger, Dana Sleicher, David D. Maron, Hasan M. Shihab, Padmini D. Ranasinghe, Shauna Linn, Shonali Saha, Eric B. Bass, and Jennifer A. Haythornthwaite, "Meditation Programs for Psychological Stress and Well-being: A Systematic Review and Meta-analysis. *JAMA Internal Medicine,* 2014 174(3), 357–368, https://doi.org/10.1001/jamainternmed.2013.13018.

- How can you incorporate the principles of meditation into your daily routine, such as during commutes, at lunch breaks, or before bed?
- What are some specific scriptures that you can meditate on this week, and how can you apply them to your life?

# 23

# Sharing Your Faith

## Living as a Testimony and Using Scripture to Inspire Others

During high school, I naturally spoke about my faith. It was a significant part of my life, so it often came up in conversations with friends. In my first year of high school, I made great friendships, and as we moved into the second year, many of us remained together in the same class.

That year, I left Brazil for an exchange program in Jackson Hole, Wyoming, where I became a junior in high school. It was an incredible experience living with a family that taught me so much and embraced me as one of their own. But when I returned home, I had only one semester left to finish high school. Reuniting with my classmates was a joy, as many of my closest friends were still in the same class.

But not long after my return, something unexpected happened.

One of my friends, who had always been playful and lighthearted, came up to me and asked for a copy of the Book of Mormon.

I was surprised. I had talked about the gospel often, invited others to activities, and even shared my testimony with many people before.

But I never expected him to be the one to ask. Not because I doubted his goodness, but simply because he was always joking around, full of energy and laughter. It hadn't crossed my mind that he had been listening so intently all along.

With great joy, I gave him a copy of the Book of Mormon, along with a personal dedication. Some of my friends from church also wrote messages in it. We highlighted Moroni 10:3–5, inviting him to read, ponder, and pray about its truth.

A few days later, my phone rang.

It was him. But this time, he wasn't joking. He was emotional—his voice full of sincerity.

"I received an answer," he told me. "I know the Book of Mormon is true."

Tears filled my eyes as I listened.

Soon after, he started attending church, taking the missionary lessons, and embracing the restored gospel. He was baptized, made incredible friendships in the Church, attended institute, and prepared himself to serve a mission. He went on to serve honorably, and later, he met a wonderful woman of faith, got married, and built a beautiful family together.

I often look back and wonder—what if I had never shared my faith? What if I had never talked about what I believed in, simply assuming no one was interested?

But I did.

And the Lord had already been preparing his heart long before I realized it.

## An Extraordinary Friendship in College

After finishing high school, I started studying advertising, working during the day and attending college at night. It was a busy and demanding schedule, but one of the greatest blessings of that time was meeting an extraordinary person who would become one of my closest friends.

From the very beginning, she understood my way of living—my passion for the gospel, the Church, and especially our Lord and Savior, Jesus Christ. Our friendship was effortless, filled with mutual respect and admiration. Whenever I shared details about my faith, whether about church activities or institute classes, she listened with genuine interest.

I explained to her how our institute classes worked—each year, we focused on a different book of scripture, diving deep into the Old Testament, New Testament, the Book of Mormon, and Doctrine and Covenants. After the classes, we often had church dances, which I told her were always so much fun. She understood that my faith was something that brought light into my life, but she also saw its depth. It wasn't just about the activities but about something truly meaningful to me.

## A Friend Who Inspired Me

One of the reasons our friendship was so special was that I looked up to her in many ways. She was incredibly dedicated to her family, always making time for them despite her busy schedule. She was a problem-solver, always willing to help me or others whenever we needed anything. She gave me rides when I needed them, was incredibly understanding, and had a way of making others feel at ease.

I admired her in so many ways. She was intelligent, professional, and had a natural ability to handle complex situations.

## A Tragic Loss That Changed Everything

Then, unexpectedly, tragedy struck.

Her father passed away suddenly from a heart attack. There had been no warning signs. One moment, life was normal, and the next, everything had changed.

In the midst of overwhelming grief, she became the rock of her family.

This loss left a mark on her heart, and it opened a space for new questions—questions about eternity, about where he was, about what came after this life.

## The Lord Had Been Preparing Her

When I returned home from my full-time mission, I reconnected with her, and something was different.

She was more open, more willing to hear about the gospel. Not because I had convinced her, but because she had lived through experiences that made her seek for something more.

A few months later, she was baptized.

She later met a wonderful man, and together, they built a strong foundation. They got married and sealed in the temple, creating a family built on gospel principles.

## Encouragement for Those Hesitant to Share Their Faith

I know that sometimes sharing the gospel can feel intimidating.

I remember when I was a teenager, sitting in sacrament meeting on a fast Sunday, listening to members of my ward share their testimonies. One brother stood up and spoke with such certainty and conviction that it caught my attention.

I wanted to have that same certainty.

Later, I remembered something that missionaries always taught: "If you want to know the Book of Mormon is true, read it. And then ask God with a sincere heart, with real intent, and He will answer you."

And He did.

And that's when I understood something: We naturally share the things we love.

If we have felt the peace, joy, and guidance that come from following Jesus Christ, why wouldn't we want to share that with others?

If you have ever hesitated to share your testimony, I encourage you—open your mouth. Just be yourself.

## The Power of Sharing the Gospel

President Russell M. Nelson taught: "Anytime you do anything that helps anyone . . . take a step toward making covenants with God, . . . you are helping to gather Israel."

The Savior Himself gave us this commission: "Go ye therefore, and teach all nations, baptizing them in the name of the Father, and of the Son, and of the Holy Ghost."[81]

---

81. Matthew 28:19–20.

We don't need to preach with loud voices. Instead, we can share the gospel simply by living it: "Therefore, hold up your light that it may shine unto the world."[82]

So, if you ever wonder whether sharing your faith is worth it, remember that you are planting seeds that God will water in His own time.

*Laís Gonçalves*

## Questions to Ponder

- Have I ever considered that my daily conversations—simple, casual, unplanned—might be planting seeds of faith in someone's heart? How can I be more intentional in allowing my love for the gospel to naturally shine through?
- What moments in my life have strengthened my testimony the most? How can I use those experiences to uplift and inspire others without fear or hesitation?
- How do I respond when someone around me is going through a difficult time? Do I offer them the hope that the gospel brings, or do I hold back? How can I be a better instrument in God's hands during someone's searching season?
- When have I personally felt the Lord preparing me for something greater, even before I understood why? How does this help me trust that He is also preparing others around me to receive the truth when the time is right?

82. 3 Nephi 18:24.

# 24

# Conclusion: A Life Aligned with Scripture

## Sustaining Growth and Encouraging Others to Live by Scripture

Scriptures are more than just words on a page. They are living, breathing messages from God—messages meant to guide us in every facet of our lives. From overcoming anxiety to navigating change, building stronger families, and developing personal discipline, each story reveals a powerful truth. Aligning our lives with the teachings of Jesus Christ brings peace, purpose, and lasting joy.

Growth is not a one-time event; it's an ongoing process. As we've seen in Caroline's journey of learning to balance work and rest, in Ana's experience of finding healing through forgiveness, in Letícia's unwavering commitment to gratitude, and in Laís's faith while facing personal trials, spiritual progress comes step by step. The scriptures teach us that our growth often comes "line upon line, precept upon precept."[83] This incremental process requires patience and faith.

83. 2 Nephi 28:30.

Sometimes we may not recognize our own progress until we look back and see how far we've come.

Living a scripture-aligned life means allowing the word of God to become the framework for our decisions, priorities, and even our daily routines. As President Russell M. Nelson counseled:

"I plead with you to make time for the Lord!"[84]

"If you don't yet love to attend the temple, go more often—not less."[85]

We could even add:

"If you don't yet love to study the scriptures, study them more—not less."

"If you don't yet love to pray, pray more—not less."

## Living a Christ-Centered Life

A life aligned with scripture is ultimately a life centered on Jesus Christ. His teachings give us direction, His Atonement offers us hope, and His example shows us how to serve, love, and grow. By following Christ's example, we learn the importance of humility, compassion, and faithfulness.

President Ezra Taft Benson taught: "When we put God first, all other things fall into their proper place or drop out of our lives."[86]

Christ-centered living brings clarity amid confusion, and strength during trials. His teachings are not simply guidelines for when life is comfortable; they are the foundation that holds us steady when life feels overwhelming. When we face loss, disappointment, or hardship, the words of Christ remind us that we are never alone. As we trust in His promises, we find peace that surpasses understanding.

---

84. President Russell M. Nelson, *Make Time for the Lord*, General Conference (Salt Lake City: The Church of Jesus Christ of Latter-day Saints), October 2021, Gospel Library App.

85. President Russell M. Nelson, *The Temple and Your Spiritual Foundation*, General Conference (Salt Lake City: The Church of Jesus Christ of Latter-day Saints), October 2021, Gospel Library App.

86. President Ezra Taft Benson, *The Great Commandment—Love the Lord*, General Conference (Salt Lake City: The Church of Jesus Christ of Latter-day Saints), April 1988, Gospel Library App.

## The Power of Daily Choices

Sustaining spiritual growth comes from small, consistent acts of faith—prayer, scripture study, service, and obedience. These choices create habits that strengthen our relationship with the Savior. As Elder Dieter F. Uchtdorf counseled: "Exaltation is our goal; discipleship is our journey."[87]

Every choice to follow Christ shapes who we are becoming. Even in times of struggle or uncertainty, holding fast to His word will keep us grounded. Daily choices like forgiving others, speaking kindly, and extending love make an eternal difference. It is through these seemingly simple acts of discipleship that our character is refined.

## Encouraging Others by Example

A life aligned with scripture naturally influences those around us. As the Savior said: "Ye are the light of the world."[88]

When we live by scripture, our example invites others to experience the same peace and purpose that comes from following Christ. Sharing the gospel through our actions with kindness, generosity, forgiveness, and patience is one of the greatest ways to lead others to Him. Our willingness to live by faith, even when it is challenging, demonstrates the power and joy of a Christ-centered life.

## Moving Forward with Faith

A life centered on Jesus Christ is one of trust—trust that His promises are sure, that He knows our needs, and that His plan for us is greater than anything we could create on our own. President Thomas S. Monson wisely counseled:

"Decisions do determine destiny." [89]

---

87. Dieter F. Uchtdorf, *It Works Wonderfully!*, General Conference (Salt Lake City: The Church of Jesus Christ of Latter-day Saints), October 2015, Gospel Library App.

88. Matthew 5:14.

89. President Thomas S. Monson, *The three Rs of Choice*, General Conference (Salt Lake City: The Church of Jesus Christ of Latter-day Saints), October 2010, Gospel Library App.

"May we ever choose the harder right instead of the easier wrong."[90]

Choosing to align your life with Christ's teachings will require effort, but it will also bring peace, purpose, and a sense of belonging in His eternal plan. The courage to stand for truth and righteousness, even when the world's standards differ, is a testament of our commitment to the gospel.

## Questions to Ponder

We invite you to reflect on these questions:

- How can you more fully center your life on Jesus Christ?
- What daily habits can you develop to draw closer to Him?
- Who in your life might be blessed by your example of living the gospel?

May you continue to find strength, clarity, and peace as you align your life with the scriptures. As you do, you will not only experience personal growth but also bless and uplift those around you. The Lord's promise is sure: "Draw near unto me and I will draw near unto you."[91]

This is the heart of a life aligned with scripture—a life that draws closer to the Savior, Jesus Christ, whose love and guidance will sustain you through every season of your journey. Let your light shine by embracing His teachings and sharing His love. In doing so, you fulfill the divine purpose God has for you and help bring others unto Christ.

---

90. President Thomas S. Monson, *Choices*, General Conference (Salt Lake City: The Church of Jesus Christ of Latter-day Saints), April 2016, Gospel Library App.

91. Doctrine and Covenants 88:63.

# About the Authors

Ana Carolina de Castro is one of the founders and co-hosts of the *MartaMaria* Podcast. She loves teaching the gospel in an authentic, fun, and lighthearted way, helping others feel God's love in their daily lives.

A devoted member of The Church of Jesus Christ of Latter-day Saints, Ana served as a missionary on Temple Square, where she shared the gospel with people from all over the world. She has also served in numerous church callings, supporting individuals and families in their spiritual and personal growth. Her deep understanding of faith, service, and community shines through in her work, making her a trusted voice for those seeking inspiration and encouragement.

Originally from Brazil, Ana now resides in the Utah with her children. As a mother, she understands the challenges of balancing personal and professional responsibilities and finds joy in teaching, creating meaningful content, and connecting with others. When she's not working on the podcast or serving in her community, she enjoys traveling, reading, and exploring new cultures.

Caroline Melazzo is a dedicated real estate agent, podcaster, and co-author of *The Not-So-Secret Life of Real Mormon Wives.* With a bachelor's degree in business administration, she brings a unique perspective to her writing and discussions. Caroline's leadership experience as a former Relief Society president, along with her husband's calling as a bishop in the Portuguese ward in Utah, has deepened her understanding of community, service, and the everyday experiences of modern women within The Church of Jesus Christ of Latter-day Saints.

The profound loss of her parents has also shaped her perspective, strengthening her belief in the eternal nature of families and the comfort faith provides during difficult times. This belief is central to her work, as Caroline explores the intersection of faith and personal growth.

In addition to contributing to the book, Caroline is one of the co-hosts and founders of the podcast *Marta Maria.*

Whether through her writing or podcast, Caroline's approach is centered on empowering others to strengthen their faith, build strong families, and navigate the challenges of life with grace and purpose.

Laís Freire de Carvalho Gonçalves is a wife, mother of three, and a passionate storyteller. She has been married to Artur for over a decade, and together they have built a life centered on faith, family, and purpose. Born into a family where her parents were the first converts to The Church of Jesus Christ of Latter-day Saints, Laís is the youngest of three siblings and deeply values the foundation of faith, resilience, and love she learned from her parents and older brothers. She served as a missionary in the Brazil Cuiabá Mission from 2012 to 2014, an experience that strengthened her testimony and deepened her love for sharing the gospel.

She is one of the founders and co-hosts of the *MartaMaria* podcast, Professionally, Laís works as a social media manager and personal assistant, helping businesses and individuals bring their vision to life. Her academic journey includes studies in education and advertising, both of which have shaped her passion for communication, organization, and creativity.

Through her writing, podcast, and daily interactions, Laís seeks to inspire others to find strength in faith and embrace God's unique plan for them. She believes that life's challenges and blessings serve a greater purpose and that every story has the power to uplift and inspire.

Leticia Araujo is a passionate communicator, entrepreneur, and co-host of the *MartaMaria* podcast. With a background in visual communications, Leticia has worked extensively in marketing, data analysis, and design. Her professional experience includes years of work in email marketing and social media management, as well as a role in international marketing where she specialized in data analysis.

Born and raised in São Paulo, Brazil, Leticia married her husband there before moving to the United States, where they have built a life together with their two children. Deeply committed to sharing the gospel, Leticia believes that defending and promoting God's truth is part of her life's mission. Whether through podcasting, writing, or community service, she strives to help others feel God's love in their daily lives.

In her free time, Leticia enjoys freelancing design projects, and editing podcast content—always finding joy in using her talents to support others.

THE *MARTAMARIA* PODCAST IS A PLATFORM DEDICATED TO PROVIDING uplifting and faith-centered content to Portuguese-speaking audiences worldwide. Through insightful discussions and gospel-centered conversations, the *MartaMaria* podcast has built a strong online presence, connecting with thousands of listeners across Brazil, Africa, and Portugal.

The podcast focuses on Christian and religious topics, including discussions on the *Come, Follow Me* program, offering listeners a space for spiritual growth and reflection. Weekly, the hosts dive into scripture, provide thoughtful commentary, and explore the practical applications of faith in daily life, creating an engaging and welcoming space for listeners to deepen their understanding of the gospel of Jesus Christ.

With personal insights, gospel principles, and meaningful discussions to help others draw closer to Christ and find strength in their own journeys, the hosts share their love for the scriptures and their desire to inspire listeners in every episode. Tune in weekly to hear from special guests with unique backgrounds offering one of a kind perspectives to further enhance your *Come, Follow Me* study.

Scan to find MartaMaria on Youtube

Scan to find MartaMaria on Instagram

Scan to find MartaMaria on Spotify